The New Supervisor's Survival Manual

The New Supervisor's Survival Manual

William A. Salmon

AMACOM

American Management Association

New York • Atlanta • Boston • Chicago • Kansas City • San Francisco • Washington, D.C.
Brussels • Mexico City • Tokyo • Toronto

This publication is designed to provide accurate and authoritative information in regard to the subject matter covered. It is sold with the understanding that the publisher is not engaged in rendering legal, accounting, or other professional service. If legal advice or other expert assistance is required, the services of a competent professional person should be sought.

Library of Congress Cataloging-in-Publication Data
Salmon, William A.
    The new supervisor's survival manual / William A. Salmon.
        p. cm.
    Includes index.
    ISBN 0-8144-7027-0
    1. Supervision of employees—Handbooks, manuals, etc. I. Title.
HF5549.12.S24   1998
658.3'02—dc21   98–8085
                                                CIP

Printing number

20 19 18 17 16 15 14

Contents

Introduction: The Role of a Supervisor   1

1   The Challenge of Being a Supervisor   9

2   Understanding What's Expected of You   22

3   Learning Written and Unwritten Rules   39

4   Motivation: Getting Commitment
    From Others   57

5   Setting Goals and Priorities   74

6   Communication   93

7   Delegation   109

8   Decision Making   127

9   Problem Solving   145

10 Coaching and Feedback   166

11 Performance Appraisal and Development   189

12 Conducting Effective Meetings   214

13 Evaluating and Managing Your
    Own Performance   232

Index   243

To
Rosemary:
In sickness and in health

Introduction:
The Role of a Supervisor

Everyone has his own specific vocation or mission in life. Everyone must carry out a concrete assignment that demands fulfillment. Thus everyone's task is as unique as his specific opportunity to implement it.

—Victor Frankl, renowned psychiatrist and Holocaust survivor

Congratulations on your promotion to supervision!

In the next few months, your new position will bring you many rewards, challenges, and opportunities. Much of what you will be doing now will be a natural extension of your past successes. Some situations, however, will require different skills and new approaches. This book has been written to help you get started on the right foot, headed in the right direction.

Many successful supervisors look back on the first few months of their new job as the most critical time in their careers. Your own success will depend largely on your ability to:

- Establish and maintain high performance standards for yourself and for others.
- Communicate effectively at all levels of the organization.
- Request and respond to feedback from employees who report to you.
- Establish clear expectations and priorities.
- Resolve open issues decisively.

- Take ownership of and accountability for your actions and decisions.
- Establish effective, two-way communication with your manager.
- Recognize the significance of your role as a member of your company's management team.
- Understand how your actions affect every employee you interact with every day.

In your previous position as an individual contributor, lines of communication were fairly straightforward and usually upward. Your immediate supervisor was your main source of information, and most of your work-related conversations probably focused on effective two-way communication with that one key individual.

Before your promotion, lateral communication was probably easier, too. You probably maintained positive relationships with a handful of coworkers who had the biggest effect on the work you were doing. Now, in your supervisory position, you may find it difficult, at first, to figure out new alliances, to determine which peers will have the greatest impact on your performance, and to decide which lateral links you need to make or maintain in order to strengthen your team's chain of communication. Sandra M. Ward, human resource manager for Vermont Yankee Nuclear Power Corporation, encourages new supervisors to be patient with their changing situation:

> Whenever I talk to new supervisors, I want them to know they will feel uncomfortable and "in-the-middle" for a while during their transition to a supervisory position. I caution them that past allegiances and alliances may not work the same now. Relationships may have changed when their promotions were announced. I encourage them not to assume things have stayed the same, and I recommend that they keep an open mind and ask questions because adjustments may be necessary. I tell them that persistence and perseverance are essential qualities of a good supervisor, and I remind them that there is a strong support system in the company available to help them succeed.

Things have changed now, and you may be at the center of a number of crisscrossing communication channels:

- Between your employees
- Between your manager and your employees
- Between peers or coworkers
- Between other internal or external resources who work with or for your department

Many new supervisors have described this phenomenon as "life in the buffer zone," caught in the middle between differing points of view and conflicting expectations. In some cases, you may feel as if you have parachuted into a foreign land where everyone speaks a unique and different language. You are their interpreter, and your mission is to make sure everyone understands everyone else. Quite a challenge!

Although the words may never be spoken, everyone will want to know whose side you are on, and they will watch how well you balance opposing opinions and how far you lean toward one side or the other. In fact, you have crossed an imaginary line and joined a new team: You have become a *member* of your company's management team and the *leader* of your own work team. You will be helping to set standards rather than living up to performance goals set by others. You will be held accountable for what may seem, at times, to be contradictory outcomes: meeting your manager's expectations and keeping your employees satisfied and productive.

Now, if employees use "we/they" language to describe what is going on in your work area, you often will not be (and cannot be) a part of the "we" group. You are a member of the team usually described as "they" whenever employees are disgruntled and need to blame someone else by saying, "What do *they* expect from us now?" or "Why don't *they* ever ask us for our opinion?" You are now part of that group.

For as long as you are in a supervisory position, you have crossed that invisible line and changed the way you can and must interact with people who used to be your coworkers or peers. Most people will understand and respect the difference created by your new position. A few may not be that respectful of your supervisory duties and responsibilities. These individuals will need coaching and coaxing to help them understand your new relationship with them.

Above everything else, your employees will expect you to represent them fairly with management. If you have been promoted from their ranks, you may feel the additional pressure of having been "one of them" a few weeks ago. That gives you the unfair and difficult advantage of knowing more about them than others do, since you probably have heard firsthand some of their complaints and concerns. In fact, you may have even contributed to some of these conversations in a supportive or sympathetic way.

Meanwhile, your manager will expect you (as a new member of the management team) to represent the views of management fairly with your former coworkers and to take a different perspective on many of the same issues that you used to debate openly from the other side. This is a fair expectation that was part of your promotion package. It should not require you to abandon previous beliefs or to become a radically different person. However, it will require you to weigh other factors, take a broader look at certain situations, and communicate your decisions and opinions more carefully to a growing number of people who will have a surprisingly new level of interest in everything you have to say.

Your company's success depends on the ability of individual supervisors like you to direct and influence the job performance of their employees. In order to maintain your company's reputation and excellent tradition, you will need to recognize the critical importance of positive supervisory practices based on the following principles:

- Supervisors have the responsibility for producing desired results through others and are, therefore, ultimately accountable for the actions, behaviors, and performance results of their employees.
- Supervisors are expected to communicate effectively, to build strong work relationships, to foster teamwork, and

to demonstrate leadership ability in support of business goals.

- Supervisors must plan and organize their activities for maximum efficiency so that they can act as a catalyst for others by showing a task orientation, imparting a sense of purpose, and translating directives into meaningful challenges for others.
- Supervisors have the responsibility for making informed decisions, to take decisive action in resolving problems, and to confront individual or team performance issues in a timely, honest, and constructive way.
- Supervisors are expected to recognize the talents of others and to assist their employees in developing skills and potential through active coaching, training, counseling, and recognition of their accomplishments.
- Supervisors have the responsibility to create and maintain a work environment in which high expectations and standards of success are consistently met.
- Supervisors are expected to work effectively with their managers and their peers as members of a management team so that their collective efforts will set an example of excellence and demonstrate a commitment to quality that will be a standard for their employees, their company, and their industry.

When asked to discuss their achievements and challenges, many successful supervisors describe some or all of the following competencies. As you begin your new supervisory responsibilities, decide which of the following skills are important to you now. You may also want to check off areas for your own professional development based on the essential requirements of your new job. In order to demonstrate the supervisory practices stated above, you must have or develop the following competencies and put them to use in your daily job performance:

☑ *Planning and organizing.* Create time for planning to establish priorities, determine resources, anticipate problems, and develop contingency plans.

☐ *Interpersonal effectiveness.* Create positive working relationships and involve others in working collectively toward the achievement of business goals; collaborate with others in decision making, foster a sense of cooperation among team members, and deal effectively with conflict.

☐ *Communication.* Deliver your messages clearly and facilitate the flow of information; listen well, solicit input from others, and exchange information at all levels.

☐ *Problem solving.* Gather and analyze data to identify a problem, then select the right resources and people to deal with the situation effectively.

☐ *Decision making.* Determine the scope, importance, and urgency of your decisions and act on issues in a timely way, using good judgment based on good information.

☐ *Initiative.* Anticipate needs and take action without being asked; confront problems in order to solve them, and assume responsibility for getting things done.

☑ *Coaching.* Recognize the capabilities and talents of others and help them develop their skills and potential by giving them direction, feedback, and encouragement.

☐ *Motivation.* Create and maintain an environment in which high expectations and high standards are consistently met; generate commitment from others; create positive working relationships by encouraging others to collaborate in achieving common goals.

☐ *Risk acceptance.* Take responsibility for successes or failures and deal proactively to avert mistakes; take action when apparent benefits outweigh potential costs or risks.

☑ *Delegation.* Assign tasks to appropriate employees, encourage employees to take responsibility for their work, and share your authority with them.

☐ *Setting goals and priorities.* Define and communicate realistic goals that are compatible with company and departmental objectives, determine and assign priorities, and achieve goals on time and within budget.

☐ *Efficiency.* Successfully structure tasks to meet deadlines;

manage personal time, establish priorities, and oversee
work projects and costs through careful follow-up.

☐ *Credibility.* Deliver on commitments and take responsibility for the results of your actions; be seen as a person who
is honest, responsive, reliable, consistent, and informed.

☑ *Time management.* Use time wisely, prioritize and schedule tasks effectively; complete work within established
time frames and eliminate your own time wasters.

☐ *Team building.* Create cooperation and teamwork to improve individual and group effectiveness; clearly communicate goals, roles, and responsibilities; remove barriers to team effectiveness.

☑ *Performance management.* Establish performance goals
with employees; observe performance and provide
timely feedback; prepare honest and thorough performance-based evaluations.

☐ *Flexibility.* Be ready and willing to adapt to change; demonstrate tolerance for changing or uncertain situations;
use different approaches depending on different situational factors.

☐ *Innovation.* Develop creative ideas and approaches for
performing tasks, making decisions, or resolving problems; look for better ways to get the job done.

☐ *Meeting management.* Use meetings as an effective way to
communicate information consistently and to collect
ideas from your team about important problems or issues.

☐ *Service to customers.* Know the needs of internal and external customers; act in the customer's best interest;
show concern for the customer's pressures, problems,
and priorities; measure quality of service and satisfaction
from the customer's perspective.

This book has been designed to help you move smoothly
and comfortably into your new leadership role. It has been developed to supplement the formal training programs you may
attend at some later date. There are thirteen chapters: one for
each of the twelve key skills new supervisors often describe as

critical to them in their new job and a final chapter on self-assessment. Reading the material and trying some of the application exercises will take only thirty to forty-five minutes per chapter.

Chapters 1 through 3 focus on the job of supervision and what you need to know immediately to get off on the right foot. Chapter 4 looks at motivation and describes ways in which you can get commitment from others. Chapter 5 includes techniques and skills related to understanding and defining priorities and communicating your expectations. Chapter 6 is devoted to communication skills, and Chapter 7 focuses on delegating projects and other work assignments. Chapters 8 and 9 emphasize two common supervisory activities: making decisions and solving problems. Chapter 10 focuses on what many supervisors consider the most difficult part of their job: giving honest and accurate feedback about someone else's performance. Chapter 11 provides useful information about ways to evaluate the performance of others and create individual development plans to improve current skills. Chapter 12 recommends ways to conduct effective meetings, and Chapter 13 provides checklists for ongoing self-assessment.

The suggestions included in this book are based on years of practical experience collected from people who have been in your situation during their careers. We hope you find this "how-to" information helpful, easy to use, and valuable to you in your new job.

1 | The Challenge of Being a Supervisor

You will never stub your toe standing still. The faster you go, the more chance there is of stubbing your toe, but the more chance you have of getting somewhere.

—Charles Kettering, former president of General Motors

In your previous nonsupervisory position, your major concern was achieving whatever results the company expected from you as an individual contributor. To do this successfully, you probably reviewed goals, desired outcomes, and performance standards with your manager. Then, all you had to be concerned with was your own job performance: Were you doing enough quality work in a timely way at a reasonable cost?

No doubt, you took a great deal of pride in your work, held yourself accountable for excellent results, and demonstrated exemplary work habits. Your individual contributions made life easier for your supervisor, and you were rewarded regularly in ways that made you willing to continue doing a good job for yourself and for the company.

Recently, you were rewarded in a different way for your hard work and conscientious performance. Your promotion to this supervisory position is a form of recognition reserved for select individuals who have demonstrated the talent and the potential to lead others. This special recognition also brings with it some new responsibilities, such as:

9

- Sharing your expertise and even your favorite projects.
- Setting a good example for others.
- Planning and coordinating activities with other departments.
- Using different criteria to evaluate your own job performance.
- Observing and evaluating the performance of those employees who report to you.
- Identifying methods for improving the efficiency and effectiveness of various processes.

You now play an important role in the lives of the people who report to you. By helping them do a good job and being accessible to them when they need your help, you are in a position to influence their sense of security, accomplishment, and self-esteem. One of the most important initial challenges facing you is how to use the authority or power that has been entrusted to you by your organization.

A common definition of power is "the ability to influence others to act or respond in a particular way, to get things done the way the person with power wants them done." For many of us, the word *power* has a negative connotation; we associate it with the misuse or abuse of power in a manipulative or egotistical way. We have all known bullies; we have all read about tyrants and dictators; we can all name people who have exploited others and used their authority to intimidate, coerce, or control. We talk about "power plays"—those situations in which certain people have flexed their muscles and overpowered others with their words, their organizational connections, or their threats of retaliation. Many of us are so uncomfortable with these negative examples of aggressive power that we have a difficult time seeing power as the basis for viable, positive supervisory action within our organization.

However, most people have some degree of power. It can come from several possible sources:

- The position they hold in the company
- Their personal qualities, talents, and experiences
- The information they can access

- The resources they control
- The relationships they have developed with others

Take a few minutes to consider the nature and source of the power you currently have in your organization:

- *Position power* is based on any legitimate authority associated with your job. For example, you now influence others because you have the legitimate authority to enforce company policies and because you have some say about organizational rewards such as pay increases, promotions, challenging work assignments, and other forms of recognition.
- *Personal power* comes from those qualities, traits, or practices that allow you to influence the behavior of others. Sometimes this type of power is based on specific expertise or special knowledge. Sometimes it comes from personal qualities that we usually describe with admiring words like charisma, charm, integrity, or credibility. Personal power enables you to influence others because they like you, trust you, or believe in you. People will follow your example, go along with you, or accept what you recommend because they really have no reason to resist. That makes you "irresistible" in a positive sense of the word.
- *Information power* comes from your ability to help others deal with confusion or uncertainty. In your supervisory position, you will be expected to know more about your company's goals and strategies and about your company's "unwritten rules" than your employees do. You will be "in the know," and you will have the power to make choices about how you use information—to improve relationships or to isolate yourself from others who can benefit from what you know.
- *Resource power* comes from your ability to access or control resources, especially time, money, and people. The scarcer the resource, the more power you have. The amount of financial signing authority a person has is often a good indicator of that person's resource power. If you need to get your supervisor's authorization to buy a $50 tool, you have less resource power than someone who can select and purchase a new computer without needing to ask for approval. The person who de-

termines the budget and establishes spending restrictions usually has more power than the person who actually spends the money. The person who sponsors a project team or authorizes certain individuals to participate and give their time to the effort usually has more resource power than the project team leader or the team members.

- *Relationship power* is based on the individual contacts you have made and maintained. The more connections you have with the right people, the stronger your base of power. If you have developed a network of peers, customers, managers, suppliers, and key employees at all levels of your organization, then you have enhanced your relationship power. The challenge is determining who the *right* people are, how much time you can afford to dedicate to building strong working relationships with others, and what you are able to bring to these relationships that will be useful to the other person. Time is such a precious resource when you are at work that you need to be both honest and selective about these "partnering" activities. Two questions can help: "How can this person I am making or keeping contact with help me or my team be more productive, effective, or efficient?" and "What information, resource, support, or help can I reciprocate with that will make this relationship beneficial to the other person?"

Using Your Power Effectively

First line supervisors have several roles in our company. They need to confront the anxiety and fears that come with change. They need to be effective communicators, aligning every employee with the company's goals. They need to empower people and make them proud to be a part of this incredible company we're building. And finally, first line supervisors need to enable greatness, to create for each employee the opportunity to contribute to what we must build in the years ahead.

**John P. Mulroney, president and chief operating officer,
Rohm and Haas Company**

How you use the power that is available to you in your new position will determine how successful you are at leading the team you now supervise. The first step in deciding how to use your power effectively is to identify the amount of authority you now have in specific situations. Your base of power will probably change as you get more experience and demonstrate greater competence and confidence in your new supervisory position. But for now, use the following chart to clarify how much power or authority you have to perform some of your current supervisory responsibilities. For example, where on the chart would you put activities like hiring a new employee, firing someone who works for you, organizing a routine project, scheduling work assignments, approving a leave of absence, authorizing overtime, or sending someone home from work because of a safety violation? List these and as many other responsibilities as you can think of in the appropriate spaces below:

Level 3: Complete authority (I make the decision and keep my manager informed.)

_____

_____

_____

Level 2: Some authority (I discuss my decision with my manager before acting.)

_____

_____

_____

Level 1: Limited authority (my manager handles this with some input from me.)

_____

_____

_____

Level 0: No authority (my manager handles this most of the time and lets me know.)

_____

_____

_____

If you have questions about your current level of authority, talk things over with your manager so that you are clear about how much autonomy you have in these situations.

One of the first things you must learn is that you cannot (and should not) do everything yourself. You will have to determine how to get results through others—which is often the way successful supervisors define their job. Your new job will require new skills, new approaches, and new ideas. Tony Barth, learning and development manager for an international chemical company, believes that new supervisors need to "develop the appropriate knowledge and skills to work effectively with people, to balance their concern for people and for results." John Horan, controller for the Miller Curtain Company in San Antonio, has a similar perspective:

> Forget the stereotypes you may have heard about how a boss should act. Function less like a drill sergeant and more like a high school football coach. Involve all the relevant members of your staff in any decision that affects them, but know ultimately that responsibility for any decision is yours and yours alone. Understand that the technical ability that led to your promotion is less important now than other skills—like listening, teaching, coaching, criticizing constructively—which are more subjective, less-defined, and more difficult to master.

In fact, a sports analogy may help you look at this challenge as an evolutionary process. In the past, you were a star player, a top contributor to your team's success. Now, you are a player-coach, watching from the sidelines, offering strong encouragement to your team, putting yourself into the day-to-day action strategically (and only when it is crucial for you to make a unique, individual contribution). Eventually, you will spend less and less of your time doing what you used to do. Coaching (supervision) will become an increasingly important part of your job. Your team will reap the benefits of your experience and expertise, and you will know the satisfaction of helping others succeed in their work efforts. Their performance records will reflect how well you have learned to play and enjoy your role as supervisor.

The Work of Supervision

Whenever a person experiences a shift in performance expectations and faces the beginning of the learning curve all over again, fears and anxieties are a natural part of the process. New supervisors experience the added dimension of not knowing how to relate to co-workers who just yesterday were peers, lunch buddies, and friends. In the absence of an effective transition process, is it any wonder that new supervisors often go back to doing what they feel comfortable and confident doing instead of what they are expected to be doing as supervisors? We can only expect optimal performance from new supervisors if we provide them with the necessary tools to make a successful transition.

Johanna Zitto, president, JZ Consulting & Training, Inc.

When asked to describe the duties associated with the job of a first-line supervisor, most managers and executives agree on the following "top ten" list:

1. Determine priorities.
2. Schedule and distribute work.
3. Coordinate the efforts of others.
4. Observe and evaluate employees' performance.
5. Give accurate and honest performance-based feedback.
6. Coach and train employees.

7. Handle administrative duties and relevant paperwork.
8. Communicate clearly about policies, procedures, and processes.
9. Address problems and conflicts in a timely manner.
10. Look for ways to improve the way work gets done.

Additionally, most successful supervisors describe the following responsibilities as the key components of their position:

1. Getting the required work done safely, on time, and within existing operational policies, quality standards, and budget guidelines
2. Getting work done through others and depending on them for success
3. Observing and interacting with employees at their work sites
4. Supporting management expectations and doing what needs to be done to see that corporate goals are achieved
5. Treating employees fairly and consistently

More specifically, here's how three supervisors described some traditional criteria usually associated with being a good supervisor:

Mary K. (an accounting supervisor in a credit company) remembers some of the initial challenges involved with *getting results through others*.

> For me, it became critical to plan what should be accomplished using very specific target dates. Then I had to organize everyone to accomplish the desired outcomes. As a new supervisor, it was now *my* job to influence the behavior of others in the pursuit of these goals. Then I had to evaluate their performance and provide constructive feedback and appropriate training. Finally, I had to make sure I acknowledged positive performance and corrected poor performance as quickly as possible.

The most difficult hurdle for Tina S. (a field supervisor in a large computer software company) was *developing and maintaining high-performance teamwork*.

This was a talented group of individuals, and I had worked with them in the field before my promotion. Now, as their team leader, I was responsible for helping to define the team's role, purpose, operational strengths, and areas for improvement. I was the one who had to organize the resources to reach our team goals with minimum cost and maximum efficiency. It was my job to encourage these individuals to give and accept support from other team members whenever it was needed. As time went on, we learned from our mistakes and worked together to improve our overall team effectiveness. We achieved good results, but there was never room for complacency.

Tom C. (a customer service supervisor for a national pharmaceutical corporation) recalls having to play a different role in *establishing and maintaining relationships with customers.*

Prior to my promotion, I really only needed to worry about my own work and my internal customers, those people who depended on me in order to do their jobs. When I became a supervisor, I needed to have a broader perspective about all of our customers. This meant having to understand the needs and demands of other departments; responding to their needs in a timely, effective, and positive way; resolving problems that adversely affected interdepartmental relationships; and evaluating my performance and my team's level of success from the customers' perspective. I had to keep the big picture in sight whenever I made a decision.

As you begin the important work of supervising others, these brief comments will, we hope, help you establish a frame of reference about the key skills and behaviors you will need if you are to succeed. These words of experience come from people who have been in your shoes at one time in their careers. They define the role of a supervisor by using three traditional criteria:

1. The ability to get results through others
2. The ability to establish and maintain high-performance teamwork
3. The ability to establish and maintain effective relationships with employees, coworkers, managers, and customers

Remember to keep lines of communication open. Brief conversations with your manager will help you stay informed about company and departmental priorities. Since your promotion, you have become a member of your company's management team. Keep in touch with your manager about any new policies, procedures, or company initiatives. Larry Serviolo, manager of organizational effectiveness for QAD, Inc., believes communication makes all the difference in a supervisor's early success:

> The key is to get to know your employees as quickly as possible. Meeting with them informs you, gives you a good view of your organization that you don't or won't get any other way. It also gives employees a feeling of importance. By asking several basic questions—What's going well? What's not going well? What would you like to see changed?—you establish credibility and create a partnership with your direct reports. You get to understand their personal aspirations and what's getting in their way of doing a good job. Start with a group meeting to give them a sense of you and what you're about, then schedule one-on-one meetings to get a better sense of their motivations, issues or concerns.

Two-way communication will also keep you informed about what is going on with your direct reports. Be receptive to early-warning signals that can help you anticipate problems and resolve issues before they become bigger problems. Regular meetings, either one-on-one or with your entire staff, will be vital to keep your staff informed. They also will provide you with opportunities to assess your team's morale and provide appropriate motivation. For Mike McCarthy, a personnel manager at Rohm and Haas, the challenge for most new supervisors is to do the job as naturally as possible:

> The people you supervise have high expectations of you in your new role. People need resources. They have needs and concerns. When new supervisors put up barriers to dialogue, people feel cut off, farther removed from the team. They feel their complaints or problems are not being heard. Be yourself, be real. Don't put on airs.

Many successful supervisors credit their early success to their personal experiences with good supervisors they have known. Many often cite instances in which they have learned what *not* to do by working with or for ineffective supervisors. Try the following exercise to help you reflect on and sort your past work experiences:

- When you think about the *best* supervisors, managers, coaches, or teachers you have ever had, how would you describe them? How did they make you feel? What made them effective? What qualities or techniques did you admire about them and aspire to in your new job as a supervisor? Think of a specific situation in which their expertise was especially beneficial to you, and describe it. Thinking about these individuals now may inspire you as you begin your new role as supervisor.

_____

_____

_____

- Now think about the *worst* supervisors, managers, coaches, or teachers you have ever had. How would you describe them? How did they make you feel? What made them ineffective? What characteristics made them difficult to work with? What supervisory practices did they use that you will try to avoid in your new job as a supervisor? Think of a specific situation in which their shortcomings were especially detrimental to you and others, and describe it. Thinking about these individuals now may remind you of things you definitely do *not* want to do as you begin your new role as supervisor.

_____

_____

_____

Before moving on to Chapter 2, take a few minutes now to complete the following brief self-assessment so that you will be able to refer to it during the next few months. There are similar journal forms at the end of each chapter, and they can provide valuable progress reports for you on the journey you have started here today.

Journal Entry   **Date:** _____

SELF-ASSESSMENT

A. Use the following scale to rate your current skill level in the areas listed below:

> **0** = No experience or skill
> **1** = Little skill
> **2** = Some skill
> **3** = High skill
> **4** = One of my greatest strengths

Rating	Duties
3	Determining priorities
4	Scheduling and distributing work
3	Coordinating the efforts of others
3	Observing and evaluating employees' performance
3	Giving accurate and honest performance-based feedback
4	Coaching and training employees
4	Handling administrative duties and relevant paperwork
3	Communicating clearly about policies and procedures
3	Addressing problems and conflicts in a timely manner
3	Looking for ways to improve the way work gets done

B. Write a brief comment about how you are currently doing in the following performance areas:

- Getting the required work done safely, on time, and within existing operational policies, quality standards, and budget guidelines

_____

- Getting work done through others and depending on them for your own success

_____

- Observing and interacting with employees at their work sites

_____

- Supporting management expectations and doing all you can to see that corporate goals are achieved

---

- Treating employees fairly and consistently

C. What specific performance areas do you want to focus on in the next few weeks or months? Be sure, for example, that you are clear about how much authority you have in those key areas you identified earlier in this chapter.

2 | Understanding What's Expected of You

Before everything else, getting ready is the secret of success.

—Henry Ford, American automobile manufacturer

It is surprising how little some people know about the companies they work for. You may have received some information from a formal orientation session when you first started working for your company, from annual reports or regular newsletters, or from informal conversations with your manager or other veteran employees. However, if you are still unsure about any of the following topics, take the responsibility for finding out as much as you can about these important facets of the company you work for:

- Its history, growth, and economic challenges
- Its current mission or purpose
- Its organizational structure, including a "big picture" perspective of how key departments relate to each other
- Its current reporting structure, including key functions and managers
- Its management philosophy as written and as practiced
- Its current products and services, as well as any that have been discontinued and any that are in development

- Its facilities, including the layout of the building in which you work and the location of any other offices or plants

Cynthia Federico, change manager for AtoHaas North America, recommends that new supervisors learn as much as they can as soon as possible:

> When you first get promoted, listen, observe, seek to understand what is expected of you. Listen to your employees and find out— What's their perspective? What kind of support do they need? Get a full perspective of the whole area in which you operate. Learn about your employees—read their files; talk to peers about their interactions with them; talk to them. Actually, it's listening, not talking, that is required at this point. Take it all in. Listening is the critical skill. You really don't know what's going on, and you won't, unless you ask good questions and listen to what others have to say.

Walt Chandler, a former banking executive who is now an associate professor at West Chester University, believes that information is the key to a new supervisor's success:

> Get to know your company's agenda. Don't assume you know what you're supposed to do. Get clarity about what your boss really wants you to accomplish, his or her expectations, issues, and priorities. Find out also how your boss wants you to communicate—meetings, memos, telephone—and how often. Stay focused and stay unbiased. Don't form any opinions for at least a month. Get an unbiased read on your direct reports by balancing a wide range of information about them: read their previous performance reviews; talk to your manager; talk to customers; talk to your peers.

To help you get to know your company's culture, ask yourself, "How do things really get done around here?" The answer to this question may reinforce ideas from the previous chapter about who has power in your organization. The answer may also give you a different perspective about your most important constituents or internal customers and help you build relationships that are mutually beneficial.

Understanding Your Manager's Expectations

Start by making your boss look good. Find out your manager's major priorities or concerns, and do your best to make a significant contribution to your department's objectives. If you are not sure about your manager's expectations, ask questions and pay attention to the things that really matter. Here are a few common problems that could have important implications for you. Jot down your reactions and, wherever necessary, get clarification from your manager:

- You are running behind schedule on an important project mostly because you are not getting the information or support you need from another department. You have tried talking to the people you deal with on a regular basis, but the problem has not been resolved. How soon would your boss like to know about this problem? What would your boss expect you to do next? *discussion prior to deadline/sched. mtng face to face c all mgrs involved —*

- There have been several unexpected expenses on one of your current assignments, and you are concerned about the budget constraints you discussed with your boss at the beginning of the project. Do you have the authority to go over budget to ensure a timely and effective outcome? Do you need your manager's permission to change specifications, get additional resources, or rearrange priorities? _____

_____

_____

- One of your key customers or constituents has asked you for special considerations on a critical project. In some ways, you see this request as compromising the quality your team typically delivers, "cutting corners" to expedite delivery of a product to one of your important customers. What would your manager expect you to do in this situation? How involved would your boss want or need to be in your decision about this problem? _____

_____

- You are spending much too much time at work trying to stay ahead of things. At first, you thought the changing demands were part of your promotion, a temporary crunch. But it has been months now since you have been able to leave work on time. You have taken work home with you almost every night, and you have worked several weekends to try to catch up on your backlog. You are concerned because you do not see an end in sight. Your typically good performance is beginning to slip. Your manager is also exceptionally busy right now, but your workload has reached crisis proportions. What would your manager expect you to do? How can your resolve this problem satisfactorily for both you and your boss? *Provide specifics on why having trouble completing work/ learn what can be delegated to free self up for non-delegated work —*

Answers to questions like these will help you understand what is important to your manager and how you can meet his or her expectations. It is important for you to know what results your boss wants you to accomplish; it is critical for you to know how your boss wants you to accomplish those results and how your boss wants you to deal with problems, obstacles, or concerns. Your work relationship with your manager is one of the most significant aspects of your job, and it requires serious and consistent attention. Get to know your manager's likes and dislikes, friends and enemies, accomplishments and challenges, wishes and worries. Discuss areas where you need clarification or additional information. Focus on topics that have the most immediate impact on your new role. If you have not already done so, you may want to ask your manager questions like:

- What percentage of my time should I be spending on the nonsupervisory, technical aspects of my job?
- Are there certain situations in which I can take action independently and other situations in which you would prefer that I meet with you before taking action?
- From your experience, what suggestions can you make that will help me start off right with my employees?
- Who else in the company should I talk to about policies, procedures, or workflow?
- How often should I update you about what's going on with my work group?

- What are the priorities you want me to concentrate on, and how do you want me to keep you informed about our progress?
- What should I be most careful about in my new job?
- What are your expectations for my performance for the next six months? for the next year?

The more you know, the better and easier it will be for you to meet or exceed your manager's expectations.

Notes From Meetings With Your Manager

Understanding Your Customers' Expectations

It is also important that you identify your key customers or major constituents and understand what they expect from you. On the left side of the following chart, list the six or se n most important people who receive some product, outcome, or information from you. Who benefits from, depends on, or expects a certain level of quality from the work that you do? Your list may include external customers, peers in other departments (internal customers), other employees who depend on you for direction or assistance, managers above you who need accurate data for strategic planning, or anyone else who would be significantly affected if you did not do your current work satisfactorily.

Then use the right side of the chart to list what these customers or constituents need from you. Each individual probably has some unique requirement. One may need timely information, and another may need thorough and careful documentation. One may want the highest quality at the best price, and another may need a quick solution at the lowest possible cost. The challenge is to determine exactly what your customers or constituents need or want from you. If you do not know for sure, the best thing to do is ask them. Then listen to what they have to say and act on the information they give you. Respond to what they tell you by building relationships based on trust, mutual respect, and a personal commitment to providing the highest possible level of performance you can. That means being the best you can be at whatever people are depending on you to do for them.

Your Key Customers/Constituents	Their Needs
1. Director / Senior Mgmt	Reports / Problem solving Information
2. Mid-level managers	Collaboration / Data
3. Supervisors (mine)	Feedback / Guidance
4. Front-line employees	Training - Policy Int / Guidance
5. VIIN personnel	Reports - Subject matter expertise
6. Patients (Veterans)	Numerous - Access to care
7. Colleagues @ other VA's	Benchmarking / collaboration

Successful supervisors recommend several ways to clarify and meet your customers' expectations:

1. *Be accessible.* Let people know how to get in touch with you whenever they need you. Having an "open-door" policy at work is not good enough if you are never in your office or work area. Let your key customers know all the ways they can contact you—telephone, E-mail, fax, beeper, personal visit—whenever they have a serious question or concern.

2. *Listen to what your customers have to say.* Pay attention. Ask questions to clarify and verify your understanding. Para-

phrase or repeat what they are telling you until you are sure you are certain you are clear about what they need.

3. *Give your customers the time they need to review their work-related problems and discuss their differences of opinion.* Every conversation you have is an opportunity for you to learn more about the key people you interact with regularly at work. Giving them your time and your attention will help you learn more about their needs, interests, and concerns—vital information for you to use in building and maintaining relationships with them.

4. *Ask for feedback about your performance from people who can give you honest, accurate, and timely information.* When you get their feedback, be appreciative and willing to act on it. If others see that you are interested in knowing what they have to tell you, two-way communication will be much easier for them and more useful for you.

5. *Ask questions when you need to clarify or expand your understanding of someone's feedback to you.* Try not to assume you know what someone means. If you are not sure, get things straightened out the first time.

6. *Keep your commitments and expect others to do the same.* Maintaining high personal standards can set an example for others and can help establish your reputation as someone who lives up to a strong code of professionalism.

7. *Develop your interpersonal skills.* Be willing to work with others toward "win-win" solutions that get you the best results while meeting the other person's needs as well.

8. *Develop a philosophy of customer service that is consistent with what your company and your manager expect from your team.*

Mike McCarthy recommends that new supervisors learn their business as thoroughly as they can:

> What you do or what you make is not enough. Find out who gets your work once the pallet or product leaves your area. Who gets it next? What do they do with it? What do they need from you? In other words, ask yourself: Who are your customers? Who are your customers' customers? Pick up the telephone and

call your customers. Visit them. Team up with your customers to meet *their* customers' needs. The more information you have, the better prepared you will be to anticipate and solve problems.

In some companies, the philosophy of customer service is that each department treats every other department as a customer. If that is the case in your organization, you do not need to have direct contact or dealings with end-user, external customers to practice high-quality customer service. If you are not directly serving these external customers, you are probably serving someone who is. Therefore, everyone in your company and on your work team has a customer. Opinions of you, your department, and your team are formed on the basis of your interactions with coworkers and customers.

Before you meet with your employees to discuss quality customer service, you may want to take a tour of "customer departments" to find out what some of your internal customers expect from you. If you have external customers, you may also want to call or visit some of them to discuss their expectations of you and your group.

Notes From Meetings With Customers

When you experience extraordinary customer service, you know how good that feels. You know that your opinion of the company that provides exemplary service is high, as is your opinion of the person who provided it. When you experience extraordinary service from a coworker, similar things happen. Your opinion of that person and his or her department goes up. You may even tell others about your positive experiences.

We all know that sometimes customers can be the most

demanding people in the world. They expect convenience, quality, individual attention, and solutions to their problems. They expect you to be pleasant, patient, and flexible—even when they are not. We know a great deal about what our customers want from us because we are customers, too. We establish relationships with companies that provide the same professional attention our customers expect from us. And we never forget the bad experiences: the defective product, the rude comment, the insensitive person.

During the next few weeks, you may want to work with your team to discuss the three questions listed below:

1. Who are our customers? If we stop doing our job, who will not be able to do their job? Which people in this organization count on us to do our job well so that they can do their jobs well? Are some of our suppliers also our customers?
2. What do our customers have a right to expect from us? Are they the same things we expect when we are a customer?
3. What is the greatest challenge we have in meeting the needs and expectations of our customers?

Notes From Discussions With Your Team About Your Customers

| |
| |

These questions will help you and your team develop a philosophy of customer service and some specific actions that will demonstrate professionalism in the way you deal with customers. The following list gives some attributes of effective customer service that you may want to discuss with your team:

Courtesy—The Overall Style of Your Interaction With a Customer

- Greet the customer in a friendly way.
- Listen attentively and get details right the first time.
- Put the customer at ease, especially when she or he is anxious, confused, or embarrassed.
- Make the customer feel important.
- Thank the customer.
- Close the conversation politely.

Competence—How Well You Know and Perform Your Job

- Understand policies and procedures. ✓ ✗
- Understand the scope and limits of your authority. ✓ ✗ ✗
- Know how to locate information people are seeking. ✓ ✗
- Be able to tell customers how long it may take to get them information ✓ ✗
- Understand when, where, and how to get help. ✓

Confidence—How You Feel About Yourself and the Way You Do Your Job

- Put your best foot forward at all times so that customers know that you know what you are doing or saying.
- Remember that you have support from others in your department and the company.
- Maintain an emotional distance so that you do not take complaints personally.
- Remember your "good" customers so that you can keep the "difficult" ones in perspective.

Respect—Earn the Respect of Others by Showing Courtesy, Competence, and Confidence

Your most challenging interactions with other people are those in which you feel a lack of respect for you or your abilities. Sometimes this lack of respect is unfair and unfounded. You may be treated inappropriately by people who do not know you or who do not give you a chance to demonstrate your skills. Often their approach is not intentional or malicious. They may be so caught up in their own problems that they don't realize how they are treating you. Customers who act aggressively may really be worried; a person who has a "know-it-all" attitude may really be embarrassed or confused.

Whatever the reason, however, when you are not treated with respect, you need to do the best you can to take charge of the situation and not let it overwhelm or discourage you. In other words, you need to maintain your self-esteem and handle the situation as professionally as you can.

Dependability—Coming Through for People Who Are Counting on You

- Don't make promises you can't keep.
- Don't make promises that "box in" someone else.
- Take ownership of your actions by using "I will" statements.
- Remember what you said you were going to do, then do it! Keep a tickler system, calendar, or to-do list nearby at all times.
- Organize your priorities by determining which tasks are most important and most urgent.
- Manage your time by identifying and addressing common time wasters.

In addition to this list of positive activities, there are a few important taboos for any customer situation that you may also want to discuss with your team:

1. Don't criticize or take shots at other departments or individuals:

   They always blow it in that department.

   Jim goofed again? I'm not surprised.

2. Don't speculate about causes if you don't really know what happened:

   It was probably a computer problem.

   I'll bet I know what happened.

Instead, make it clear that you will try to get all of the facts.

3. Don't argue with or criticize another employee in the presence of a customer.
4. Don't abandon your role as representative of your company and side with the customer:

I don't blame you. If that happened to me, I wouldn't trust anybody here either.

It is always appropriate to apologize if you or someone else has made an error. But there is no need to go overboard and abandon your loyalty to your company.

5. Don't promise things you can't deliver:

I promise you, this mistake or problem will never happen again.

Understanding Your Employees' Expectations

For many supervisors, being willing and able to listen effectively to their employees has made the difference in their early job performance. Mike McCarthy believes that good listening is essential:

Regardless of how well you know your direct reports, or how well they know you, listening is the key skill you need in your new job. You have the opportunity to change things, to make things better. If you know the people you are now supervising, you know a lot about the business and the competencies of the people who now report to you. But what you need to learn is how they feel about you and this new situation. Listen to their needs. Learn what would make things better for them and for you. Then you can pull together some kind of development plan, a list of things you can do to get and keep them on your side. This will also set the stage for future interactions. Make yourself available as a resource. Empower and enable your direct reports to do their jobs as effectively as they can. Set yourself up in a different role and get to know people as well as possible.

John Horan believes that listening is especially important when there are problems:

> Listening is important because your people are your <u>most efficient window into the workings of your group</u>. It is impossible to know everything that everyone in your group is working on at a given time. But by taking the time to sit down with your people and listening carefully you can get a good read on the status of the group. Listening is also important when dealing with discontent and morale problems. Listening, without becoming defensive or trying to solve everyone's problems for them immediately, allows group members to vent, which is sometimes all they need to do. Careful listening, especially in emotionally charged circumstances, often provides clues to unspoken concerns that may be at the root of stated concerns.

For Tony Barth, listening is the basis for all other supervisory activities:

> Take appropriate time to know what is expected of you in your role as supervisor. In other words, understand the context of your job. Take appropriate time to know your direct reports. Have two-way conversations with each person about mutual expectations. In other words, understand the people-aspect of your job. Then set unit and individual goals. Delegate and provide resources and support as needed to reach these goals. Focus on the results you and your team need to accomplish.

Finally, Larry Serviolo encourages new supervisors to ask good questions and listen carefully to the answers:

> Don't be afraid to ask for help. You don't need to know all the answers. Ask for help from your boss, your peers, your direct reports, and your customers. Listening is the foundation for motivation and innovation. You cannot motivate without listening. It gives people a sense of importance. It establishes two-way communication, lets people share their views, and gives them a sense of self-esteem. If people know you listen to their ideas, they won't be afraid to come up with new ones.

When Peg G., a manufacturing supervisor, was faced with such an opportunity recently, she took the initiative and went to bat for her team. By doing so, she won their respect early in the game. Would you have had the confidence to do the same? What would you have done in a similar situation?

Case Study

Because of some current organizational factors, Peg was having a difficult time generating excitement about increasing the quality of work in her group. A number of factors (limited resources, high volume of work, outdated systems) were creating persistent barriers to her attempts to motivate a good group of employees. Every time Peg's group came up with a good idea, someone was there ready to shoot it down. Peg had become personally frustrated by the situation, and she knew that one or two of her employees had simply resigned themselves to the fact that things would never get better.

Analysis

Before you read about Peg's approach, take a few minutes to write down some of your thoughts about how you would handle this problem.

_____

_____

_____

The Supervisor's Action

Peg began by talking to her manager (Larry) about the growing frustration she and her team were experiencing. She gave him several recent examples of times when good ideas were overlooked or not appreciated. Larry admitted that he had been so concerned about the group's backlog that he had not been paying much attention to their suggestions about ways to improve working conditions in their area. Peg said she believed the two issues went hand in hand and suggested a compromise she hoped Larry would agree to: "Give me two weeks to solicit and develop ideas from my team about ways to improve productivity. Then give me another two weeks to implement their suggestions. At the end of the month, we'll check on the backlog, and if there is *any* improvement, I would like you to come to one of my staff meetings and congratulate my employees." Larry agreed, and Peg took the challenge back to her group. They were anxious to be involved in solving a problem that had been bothering many of them for months. They were motivated by being included in making decisions that would affect them and their work.

～

Here are a few other things you can do to make sure you understand what employees expect from you in your new job:

1. Read any written material available, including:
   - Your own position description and those of your employees
   - Any policy, procedure, or safety manuals
   - Your training responsibilities for your department
   - Strategic and operational goals for the company and for your department
   - Past performance reviews of all your employees
   - Your company's Employee Benefit Handbook
   - The current collective bargaining agreement, if it applies to your employees

As you read these documents, make a list of questions and decide who can provide the best answers for you.

_____

_____

_____

2. Meet informally and individually with each employee who reports to you. Ask nonthreatening questions that will help you clarify that employee's concerns and expectations.

Without making any promises, you may want to listen so that you can find out what you can do to help that employee and what changes he or she would like to see.

Notes From Meetings With Employees

Before moving to Chapter 3, take a few minutes to summarize the key learnings you have gotten by reading available information and by talking to your manager, direct reports, and customers. List any data that will help you clarify what others expect of you as a new supervisor.

Journal Entry   **Date:** _____

1. The company I work for expects me to:

_____

_____

2. My manager expects me to:

_____

_____

3. My direct reports expect me to:

_____

_____

4. My internal customers expect me to:

_____

_____

5. My external customers expect me to:

_____

_____

6. To balance and meet all of these expectations, it will be critical for me to:

_____

_____

3 | Learning Written and Unwritten Rules

I believe the real difference between success and failure in a corporation can very often be traced to the question of how well the organization brings out the great energies and talents of its people.

—**Thomas J. Watson, Jr., former chairman, IBM**

You are your company's first-line representative. Even though you did not set your company's policies, you have to accept them and be able to explain them. Your manager will look to you to be sure these policies are followed. Whether you like them or not is immaterial. Most employees will understand that you have a responsibility to enforce company policies. On occasion, they may want you to try to change policies or procedures that seem outdated or unfair, but they will usually understand that you have limited authority to change things overnight.

Most policies and procedures establish limitations or constraints. When employees have questions about these restrictions, they will expect you to explain how certain policies benefit the company and how they apply to specific situations. Most company policies are designed to:

1. *Limit costs and expenses.* So that your company can sell its products or services competitively in today's market, certain policies regulate fringe benefits, overtime, travel expenses, va-

cation time, and other activities that have a negative effect on the company's bottom line.

2. *Ensure fairness.* In order to attract, train, and retain the best people for the available jobs, certain policies define guidelines for hiring, training, transferring, and promoting employees.

3. *Ensure consistency.* Certain policies describe acceptable procedures and practices so that supervisors handle common situations (like punctuality, attendance, and work schedules) in a fair and uniform way. Many of these policies define expectations and recommend guidelines for you and your employees to follow.

4. *Protect the company and its employees.* Certain policies related to safety (like "fitness for duty" or drug and alcohol policies) and individual rights (like sexual harassment policies) are written to ensure compliance with state or federal laws. They are based on codes of behavior designed to protect all employees from danger and discriminatory actions.

When it comes to safety procedures, most companies leave little room for discussion or debate. Rules must be followed to ensure that all employees have a safe place to work. Occasionally, however, as in the following case study, an employee may challenge the established requirements. What would you do if this happened to you?

Case Study

Richard has had a serious problem with Ed, an employee who must move in and out of areas that require hard hats and safety glasses. Ed has been with the company for about a year. After his initial training, he was careful about safety procedures. He never entered secure areas without protective clothing. However, his recent performance has become sloppy. In fact, there are times when he seems to ignore basic safety procedures. For example, about a month ago, Richard noticed that Ed was not wearing safety glasses when he was leaving the area. He immediately went to him and warned him about it.

A week later, Ed had glasses but no hard hat. Again Richard stressed the importance of the safety rules. An OSHA inspector would throw the book at him. Ed seemed to think that Richard was exaggerating about the importance of safety equipment, but he said, "Yeah, OK, I'll be more careful." Today, Richard actually observed Ed leaving a restricted area with no protective clothing. He said he only had to slip in for a few seconds, and he didn't see the point of going to all that trouble.

Analysis

Before you read Richard's approach, take a few minutes to jot down some of your thoughts about how you would deal with this situation.

_____

_____

_____

_____

_____

The Supervisor's Action

Richard met privately with Ed and stated specifically what he had observed ("You were leaving a restricted area and you were not wearing any protective clothing") and what Ed had said at the time ("It wasn't worth the trouble"). Richard then laid down the law, stating firmly that there could be no exceptions to these important safety regulations. Richard reminded Ed that they had talked before about these violations. Richard then gave Ed formal warning that future incidents would be dealt with severely. Richard had the authority to send the employee home without pay and to begin a formal disciplinary process that could lead to termination. He told Ed, therefore, that there was no room for even one more infraction.

~

Such safety issues are usually black and white, with little room for individual interpretation or negotiation. Variances usually cannot be tolerated and are often illegal. However, if there are questionable preferences, practices, or company policies that affect your work area, try to do everything you can to remove potential obstacles to your team's productivity and professionalism. If you are uncertain about what is expected, clarify any of the following aspects of your job and performance expectations for your team:

1. *Job responsibilities, duties, and performance standards.* Be able to state in specific terms what quantity and quality of work your manager expects from you and your team. If you have certain time commitments and cost restraints, make sure you understand them clearly.

2. *Behavioral guidelines.* Discuss any cautions about acceptable or unacceptable behavior in the way you do your job. For example, many companies today put a high value on teamwork and effective interpersonal relationships. If this is true in your company, you will want to know so that you and your direct reports can act accordingly.

3. *Company policies.* Be able to answer any questions your employees have about smoking, dress code, time off, overtime, benefit programs, and work schedules. Remember that most companies have both written and unwritten rules, so you may want to focus on "how things are really done around here."

4. *Departmental procedures.* Be able to discuss day-to-day operations (like schedules, routine work problems, and customer complaints) and special situations (like family emergencies, personal or sick leave, and equipment breakdowns). Take the time to find out how your manager would like you to handle minor problems, major crises, and your work relationship with each other. Find out how he or she would like to be kept informed about your work. Will your manager expect written reports, regular meetings, routine observations, informal verbal updates, or a combination of these and other techniques?

5. *Where to get help.* Identify the best resources you can go to when you need help and your manager is not around. This list of names and telephone numbers should include the person

you can go to for permission or authority to do something out of the ordinary and anyone else outside your department who has special expertise that might be useful to you in an emergency.

6. *Land mines and red alerts.* Discuss potential problems and how to solve, resolve, or avoid them. Find out what you should do when you encounter these barriers or obstacles. You may be expected to deal with a customer's complaint one way and a complaint from another department in a different way, so make sure you clarify how your manager and others want you to handle specific situations.

Certain policies and their supporting procedures will permit some discretion or flexibility in interpretation or application. This leeway is provided because the writers of policy statements know that they cannot anticipate every situation or contingency. In those cases, you can act independently within the defined range of options provided. However, you should not depart from the spirit, intent, or purpose of the policy. The opportunity for flexibility is not an excuse to ignore or violate the written policy.

There will be times when you will notice inconsistent policies or announcements that overlook certain circumstances or conditions. On these occasions, it is incumbent on you to review the situation with your manager so that you do not take actions that are detrimental to the company, your department, or other supervisors. Remember that if you permit or support actions that are not consistent with an established policy, you have set a precedent that adds a new dimension to the existing policy. Your employees will talk to others about any exception you have made. In effect, you have redefined what is acceptable and changed the standards covered by this policy. It is much better for you to discuss possible exceptions with your manager before you permit actions that may be contrary to the way your company wants things to be done.

Every organization has its own key policies and procedures. Research shows that employees often ask their supervisors for clarification about the following company guidelines. Check off any of the items below that you feel you have to know more about than you do now, and then determine the best way to get the information you need:

- ☐ Time off for vacation, sick leave, jury duty, or other personal reasons
- ☐ Salary grades, potential raises, and pay schedules
- ☐ Educational opportunities and tuition reimbursement programs or procedures
- ☐ Medical coverage for themselves and their families
- ☐ Career and promotional opportunities

Research also shows that supervisors often ask their managers for clarification about the following company guidelines. Check off any of the items below that you feel you have to know more about than you do now, and then determine the best way to get the information you need:

- ☐ The performance planning and appraisal system
- ☐ Employee grievance and disciplinary processes
- ☐ Safety policies and procedures
- ☐ Employee assistance programs or referral procedures
- ☐ Ways to recognize and reward exceptional performance: salary increases, promotions, development opportunities, letters of commendation, and special project assignments

If you are supervising a group of union employees, get a copy of the latest bargaining unit contract and read it carefully. If you are not sure what parts of the contract mean, ask for directions or advice from your human resources or personnel department. You may also want to talk to someone in management who had a hand in negotiating the contract.

Know those occasions when union employees are justified in refusing to do work and supervisors cannot take disciplinary action. Those occasions usually include:

- When there is a safety risk to oneself or to others
- When the contract specifically prohibits a certain action
- When a new assignment or change of duties was not explained completely or accurately

Familiarize yourself with the grievance process, especially the role you play as a supervisor. When you are responding to a grievance that has been filed against you, prepare for the meeting by reviewing the contract and the specific situation involved. Review other situations to see if other precedents have been established. Make notes prior to your meeting. During the meeting, let the employee or steward present the complaint. Don't interrupt. Listen and respond accurately and objectively. Don't get defensive or hostile. State your case as specifically and as nonjudgmentally as possible. If you have other questions or concerns about the contract, ask for help.

In the space below, list any other policies or procedures you feel you need to know more about, and ask your manager or your human resources staff about them, too:

_____

_____

_____

Understanding and Supporting Training Policies and Procedures

In addition to the duties and responsibilities discussed in Chapter 1, you are also responsible for the training and development of the people who report to you. Although everyone in your company has an important role in training, you are responsible for making sure that the training given to your employees qualifies them to do their work safely, effectively, and efficiently. Human resources or personnel departments have a responsibility to work with you to ensure that courses provide current, relevant, and accurate information. It is part of your new job as a supervisor to understand and support your company's training and development efforts. It is your responsibility, therefore, to ensure that your employees attend training when scheduled, participate in a constructive manner, and identify additional training needs with you.

Here are a few things you can do to demonstrate your support for training, to ensure that employees assigned to you are properly trained, and to emphasize the importance of continuous improvement:

- Develop and communicate training goals for your work group.
- Clarify expectations before employees attend training.
- Make sure employees have completed any pretraining assignments.
- Ensure that employees attend scheduled training.
- Visit classrooms and observe (or participate in) training.
- Maintain close communication with training managers to ensure that your employees are following training guidelines and procedures.
- Meet with employees after training to reinforce training concepts and inquire about program content and quality.
- Observe your employees' work practices and provide supplementary training whenever necessary.

All employees are expected to recognize the importance of training and to take personal responsibility for becoming and remaining proficient in the technical, business, and leadership skills necessary to achieve department and company goals. Training and qualification programs give you the opportunity to instill in your employees or to reinforce positive work practices associated with continuous improvement efforts. In addition to developing specific skills, designated training efforts should help your employees improve their ability and willingness to:

- Demonstrate accountability and pride of ownership for their work efforts.
- Ensure that your expectations and their work assignments are clear.
- Plan and prioritize their work efforts.
- Demonstrate high personal and professional standards.
- Resolve open issues quickly and effectively.
- Communicate effectively with all levels of the organization.
- Provide and request appropriate feedback.

- Produce quality work and ensure adequate attention to detail.
- Take prompt corrective action to resolve problems and meet changing conditions.

In your previous nonsupervisory position, you most likely focused on your company's training policies and procedures from a very narrow perspective: How can available training programs help me personally improve my current level of performance? The challenge for you now is to determine how training and development initiatives can help your employees improve their individual performance and the effectiveness of your whole team.

Setting a Good Example

In some organizations, there may be real, perceived, or potential conflicts between:

- What is *really* the right thing to do and what people feel they have a right to do
- Universal or commonly shared values and individual or personal preferences
- What people *really* deserve or have earned and what they feel they are entitled to

In your new supervisory position, it will be important for you to learn both the written and the unwritten rules so that you can behave in a way that sets a good example for your employees. In general, there are several types of behavior that are unacceptable in any company at any time. If you are sensitive to people, you will probably automatically behave appropriately. However, here are some cardinal rules to remember, act on in your daily interactions with others, and hold your employees accountable for:

1. *Do not use language that offends, belittles, or demeans any group or individual.* Use bias-free, nondiscriminatory language

that stays clear of sexist or racist comments and avoids any put-downs based on a person's nationality, age, academic background, work experience, or job title. We all have biases and prejudices that can lead to stereotypes and other unfair expectations or reactions. The first step in dealing with these biases is to understand what they are. If you find yourself making generalizations like, "All young people are only interested in getting ahead at the expense of others," or "All engineers are too detail-oriented to be concerned about the people on their work teams," you have strong biases that could interfere with your work performance if you do not take care to monitor your language and your behavior. One insensitive comment or rude action can have a powerful negative impact on your relationship with one or many individuals. You are now in a position of responsibility and authority that requires you to make sure your direct reports use appropriate language at all times.

2. *Show respect for others—their time, their space, their priorities.* Unless there is an emergency, try not to impose on others or interrupt them with problems that should be discussed by appointment. Even if your managers boast about their open-door policy, do not presume to drop in casually for something that may be perceived as unimportant or low-priority. Schedule time with your manager and other managers you need to meet with, and be sure they know the nature, scope, and importance of your agenda. Casual, small-talk meetings are appropriate if you keep them short and know when to let the other person get on with business. Remember, there may be a better time and place to discuss something that's important to you, especially if the other person seems absorbed, distracted, or energized by something else. If someone shows disrespect for your time, space, and priorities, it is your responsibility to confront the issue and suggest a better alternative, like: "Can we talk about this over lunch? I'm trying to finish this report right now," or "How about if I come to your office later this morning after I've responded to this customer's inquiry?"

3. *Don't criticize others or their ideas in public.* Be especially careful about negative feelings you have about your manager or other managers. Get to know the people you can talk to pri-

vately about your concerns, and focus your efforts on the constructive resolution of these problems. Always consider a face-to-face discussion with the person you are critical of as your first course of action. If that fails, you may want to resort to getting help, in a positive way, from your immediate manager or someone with the authority and the right intentions to assist or support you.

Your organization has its own culture, developed over the years by employees who have done things in a particular way. If you are unfamiliar with those customs or unwritten rules, you need to observe how people work with one another and determine what behaviors are acceptable. Don't compromise your own professional standards, but be aware that you may need to adapt your style or change some of your preferences in order to be effective in your company's unique culture.

Most of us have deep-seated principles that govern our behavior and dictate how we treat other people. There are commonly held values—like honesty, respect for others, fairness, and being considerate—that most people embrace and practice. Treating others well, then, is an important attribute that identifies you as someone with high professional standards and a strong commitment to the well-being of others. Caring about people is one of the cornerstones of effective supervisory performance. There are, of course, some specific challenges that may test your commitment to these principles. There is always the possibility that you will meet somebody who will want you to bend the rules too often and too far, compromise your integrity for personal gain, or participate in activities that are counterproductive. You may be faced with occasional temptations to ignore the Golden Rule. It is important that you take frequent self-assessments to ensure that you are maintaining your own high personal standards. Your good reputation depends on it.

For example, your new job will give you access to confidential or proprietary information. Remember to keep it to yourself. It is essential that you be known as a person who is trustworthy and dependable, someone who can be counted on to be diplomatic and discreet. Spreading bad news, rehashing mistakes that one of your employees has made, and making wild guesses about new strategies or approaches wastes a lot of time and can demoralize the people who report to you.

Maintain a positive perspective and don't let yourself be hooked into "doom and gloom" conversations. Although complaining is a common practice in most work settings, there is no reason why you have to condone or take part in this counterproductive activity. If there is a problem with another person or department, get it resolved and get on with your work. Let your team members know that they will feel much better if they get results rather than getting a reputation as chronic complainers.

Always be courteous and diplomatic. If you do not know basic business etiquette, take the time to learn the business manners that are acceptable in your company. Observe how key managers deal with specific social or interpersonal situations. For example, you may want to notice:

- How they say no diplomatically so that others do not interpret their resistance as negativity, lack of cooperation, or unwillingness to be flexible
- How they dress for certain meetings or occasions
- What they eat and drink (or do not eat or drink) at business luncheons
- How much time they spend listening to others and how they respond when they hear bad news or when their ideas meet with resistance or opposition

There are several other common courtesies you may want to remember, demonstrate, and encourage your employees to practice:

1. *Return phone calls and respond to E-mail messages as quickly as possible.* Although you may not have time at that moment to go into detail about a specific question or concern, acknowledging that you have received the other person's message is a simple but important business courtesy. Saying, "Thanks for your call. Can we talk later this week?" lets others know that they are important to you and that you will make time to respond to them again soon.

2. *Arrive for meetings on time.* Coming to meetings late was once a popular power play that people used to show others waiting for a meeting to start how important they were. Now, lateness is usually regarded as an inconsiderate waste of time and productivity. If you show up ten minutes late for a meeting that involves six other people, you have effectively cost your company one hour of productive work time. The later you are or the larger the meeting group, the greater the amount of time lost and the greater the aggravation you cause others. Keep an accurate, updated calendar so that you do not keep people waiting because you forgot, double-booked yourself, or underestimated the time it would take for you to finish a task before your next appointment.

3. *Answer correspondence as soon as you can, especially if it comes from one of your customers.* If you neglect this common courtesy, many of your external customers will go over your head and send a follow-up letter to someone at the top of your organization. These second-chance letters will often mention you by name as the person who failed to give satisfactory service the first time. Your internal customers may be less likely to complain to someone higher in the chain of command. But your failure to respond to one of their memos has been documented and probably filed away for future use. This CYA ("cover your anatomy") behavior is typical in situations in which there is competition for resources or pressure to complete a project for which there are unrealistic expectations.

Creating a Code of Behavior for Yourself and Your Team

Many successful supervisors I have worked with over the past twenty-five years have emphasized the importance of clarifying the word *professionalism* with their work teams. They often start with the dictionary definition. Professionalism means competence in what you do for a living and includes those procedures, standards, values, and common courtesies considered proper in dealing with people at work.

Then they go on to discuss with their direct reports the written and unwritten rules the company expects its employees to observe. *Written* rules are the policies and procedures we reviewed earlier that describe how business is done in your company. You and your team are expected to conform to these established standards. *Unwritten* rules imply a choice of behavior. As you might expect, and as you may have experienced in dealing with others at work, the choices individuals make about their language, appearance, actions, and interactions influence your impression of them. Their choices may also affect your impressions of the department or organization for which they work and how you feel about dealing with them in the future. When people's behaviors or work habits interfere with their job performance or the performance of others, they are less likely to succeed, and their colleagues are more likely to see them as having a demoralizing effect on the company or their work group.

If you and your team are behaving professionally, others can depend on you to be:

- Competent and effective in delivering required results
- Comfortable people to meet and work with
- Willing to collaborate with others by sharing information and expertise

If you and your work team have high professional standards, people can trust and respect you because you:

- Keep commitments.
- Respect confidentiality and do not spread rumors or betray personal confidences.
- Do not bad-mouth or criticize people.
- Do not compromise your own personal standards.
- Try to understand the pressures others are experiencing.
- Are problem solvers.

Encourage your direct reports to develop and commit to some professional work standards of their own. For example, you may want to discuss and get agreement about some fairly basic work behaviors. Some successful supervisors have worked with their teams to develop what they call a "code of behavior" that includes words like these:

Our customers and coworkers can count on us to:

- Observe written policies, procedures, and safety rules.
- Have a consistent attendance record.
- Be ready to get down to business when the shift or work period begins.
- Return from lunch and breaks on time.
- Get our own work accomplished accurately and on time.
- Refrain from conducting personal business during work hours.

You may want to use this example as a springboard for discussing professional behavior with your team. The results should be a code of conduct that you and they are willing to follow.

Doing your job is not just about getting the work done. It is also about building relationships for the future. Your success often depends on your ability to influence or persuade others to cooperate with you. A good place to start is in your own department. You can then expand your frame of reference to include other departments that depend on you for information or service and other departments that you depend on to get your job done.

Learn your company's rules as quickly as you can. Talk to other supervisors and veteran employees. Observe the people around you. Determine which behaviors are acceptable to your manager, your peers, and your customers. Identify factors that have helped or hindered other people in your company in the past. Try to learn how people have succeeded and how they have gotten in trouble with their superiors or peers.

Establish an honest, open relationship with your manager. Ask questions, seek advice, and listen carefully to suggestions about ways you can maintain your professionalism. Build strong relationships with your coworkers by being open and friendly. You earn the respect of others by treating them in a professional way—by showing courtesy, competence, and confidence. Your peer relationships with other supervisors are built on countless daily contacts, from informal greetings on the morning elevator ride to formal exchanges during a project team meeting. Although the spontaneous, informal exchanges are more common, they often are so spur-of-the-moment that you may miss an opportunity to create a stronger connection with some of your peers. In some cases, a simple greeting can set the stage for a more meaningful connection. For example, you can enhance your relationships with peers by:

- *Asking for advice.* "How does your group handle irate customers?"
- *Asking for an update.* "How's the Magellan project going?"
- *Discussing a problem.* "How will downsizing in the marketing department affect your project?"

In other cases, these informal contacts can be useful in establishing a more formal relationship, usually characterized by scheduling a meeting or a more in-depth discussion of something that is of mutual interest or benefit. Establishing good relationships with your peers can expedite processes, give you a different perspective on important problems, gain their support for current or future projects, and provide evidence to your manager that cooperation and teamwork are important to you. All of these behaviors are evidence that you are a true professional in the way you approach your job.

The choices you make about your language, appearance, actions, and relationships with others at work will influence others' impression of you. If you want to be known as a true professional, it is your responsibility to understand your company's written and unwritten rules about work standards and performance expectations.

Respect the people you work with and expect the same from them. Most of us want to do a good job and want to work in a comfortable, harmonious environment. It is in your own self-interest to be helpful, courteous, and cordial to others. Being considerate usually generates a positive response and can strengthen work relationships. These positive behaviors can help you establish, early in your supervisory career, a reputation as a competent and confident leader with high personal standards and high professional expectations for your work team.

Before moving on to Chapter 4, take a few minutes now to complete the following Journal Entry by summarizing some of your questions and concerns about your company's policies and procedures.

Journal Entry   **Date:** _____

1. Make a list of the key policies and procedures you need to know more about, and make sure you have (or know where to locate) these important documents.

   _____

   _____

   _____

   _____

2. Make a list of the two or three key policies or procedures you antici-pate being challenged about most by your employees. Determine the best way to respond to questions or concerns.

   _____

   _____

   _____

   _____

3. Make a list of two or three key people you may need to contact if you have questions about these key policies and procedures.

   _____

   _____

   _____

   _____

4 | Motivation: Getting Commitment From Others

You must manage as if you need your employees more than they need you.

—Peter Drucker, management guru

In the past few weeks, you have had several conversations with your manager and the employees who report to you. These meetings, we hope, have helped clarify what they expect from you in your new job. Now it is time to focus on your expectations: What do you need from others in order to perform your supervisory responsibilities effectively? There are a number of factors that will affect *what you do* (your performance objectives) and *how you do it* (your style). The following questions are intended to help you examine some of your preferences about supervision. It may be useful to write some of your first impressions in the spaces provided below.

Style-Preference Questions

1. When you think collectively about the employees who now report to you, what qualities do they have to meet your overall team objectives? Do they have special technical skills? Are they conscientious

and professional in their approach to their jobs? Do they work well
together? _____

_____

_____

2. Are there any problems in the way your group works with other
   work units or in the way group members work with one another?
   When you think about individual employees, are there any key problem areas that need immediate attention? _____

_____

_____

3. How have these employees been supervised in the past? Have they
   been given the freedom to make decisions and to work independently? Have they been allowed or encouraged to try new ideas or
   approaches? Have they needed special attention or coaching in order to perform effectively? _____

_____

_____

4. What are the key organizational factors that will affect the way you
   supervise? Is there a sense of urgency about the deadlines you
   and your team have to meet? Are certain tasks or goals more critical
   than others? _____

_____

_____

5. How have you been supervised in the past? Have there been times
   when you preferred having work delegated to you, so that you felt
   completely responsible for what you were doing? Have there been
   times when you appreciated being asked for your opinion about decisions that affected your work? Have there been times when you
   expected your supervisor to call the shots and let you know what
   you had to do? _____

_____

_____

The way you supervise will vary according to the situation and the people involved. Your style or approach will depend on your expectations, the employee's level of confidence and competence, and the quality of the working relationship you have established with that particular individual.

Because people respond differently to various approaches, it will be important for you to make sound decisions about the best style to use in different situations. Some of your employees will expect you to be near their side most of the time. Others will prefer that you let them run with things on their own as long as there are no problems or emergencies. And a few employees, because of performance difficulties, will require closer attention and more specific direction than you may want to give them.

The "player-coach" analogy from Chapter 1 can help you weigh the potential benefits and disadvantages of various approaches. For example, imagine that you have been taking tennis lessons, and today you are playing in your first real match. How much direction would you need? How closely would you like to be supervised or monitored? Where would you want your coach to be?

- One option would be *on the court* with you, even though your coach might be tempted to interfere, disrupt your performance, or even take over the game from you. After all, the coach has a good deal of technical expertise and is probably much better than you at this activity.
- Another option would be *in the stands* as a spectator— cheering you on when you deserve it, venting if poor officiating occurs, bragging about your good shots, or maybe just sitting passively if you are losing. In fact, a self-centered coach worried about his or her own reputation might sit in the stands, sharing credit for your successes, but letting you take sole responsibility for your mistakes.
- The third option is *on the sidelines* as coach, giving you timely feedback, encouragement, recognition, and support.

Most supervisors would prefer the third option, and this approach is often the most effective, even when dealing with difficult situations. For example, consider the dilemma Suzanne H. found herself dealing with early in her supervisory career. A twenty-six-year-old team leader in an engineering company, Suzanne discovered that the "sideline" coaching option worked despite her employees' best efforts to drag her into the middle of their personality conflict. As with all of the case studies in this book, the situations are real but the names are fictitious.

Case Study

Dave and Elizabeth were relatively new employees who had been working together for about six months on a special project team. They both had similar academic backgrounds and excellent technical skills. When they worked independently, each person's individual performance met all of the company's established standards for quantity, quality, and cost. However, whenever they worked together, they competed with each other for Suzanne's time and attention.

Each employee scheduled frequent meetings with Suzanne. Unfortunately, these "good news/bad news" conversations usually emphasized one person's success at the other's expense. For example, when Dave described his high level of on-time output, he usually made references to Elizabeth's slower and more cautious approach. On the other hand, when Elizabeth outlined the cost-effectiveness of her limited but high-quality results, she often reminded Suzanne about the importance of getting things done right the first time and about how Dave's sloppy work might cause problems for customers.

Suzanne knew that this feuding was not confined to her office. The project team leader and a few other team members had described this competitive behavior as counterproductive and demoralizing. Suzanne knew she needed to resolve this antagonism before it completely undermined the project team's effectiveness and further damaged the individual effectiveness of two good employees.

Analysis

Before you read about Suzanne's solution, take a few minutes to jot down some of your thoughts about this situation and how you would approach it.

_____

_____

_____

The Supervisor's Action

Suzanne decided that she needed to address this conflict as quickly as possible. She watched for an opportunity to discuss the problem, and she soon overheard Elizabeth talking to some coworkers about Dave. This gave her a specific situation she could use in an immediate meeting with Elizabeth. During the conversation, Suzanne was fairly direct about both the problem and her expectations. She started the meeting by stating:

> Elizabeth, as you know, I stopped by after your project team meeting this morning, and I was surprised to hear you making negative comments to Pat and Kris about Dave and criticizing his latest report. The outcome of this project is very important to our department. You will have a lot of visibility, and it's a great chance for you to shine. But you don't have to look good at Dave's expense. Your styles may be different, but your approaches can both be successful. You need to figure out the best way to keep an eye on your work and not let your thoughts wander to Dave's work. That's my job. So what can you do to make sure you don't bad-mouth Dave in front of other people anymore?

After a brief discussion, Suzanne summarized the agreement she wanted Elizabeth to accept:

> So are you willing to agree to take your feedback about Dave directly to Dave? Or if that's not the best thing to do, can you agree to come see me whenever you need my help with that type of conversation? That way, we can make sure Dave gets

any important feedback in a way that keeps things private and confidential. I'm sure you would expect the same type of professional treatment from others as well.

When Elizabeth agreed, Suzanne pressed for a final commitment about this issue:

I need your commitment that this will be the last time we need to talk about this issue. I could reassign you to another project, but I still believe this is the best one for you. However, I need you working well with Dave so that everyone succeeds. Let's give it another try for the next few weeks, and let's agree to meet again early next month, unless another problem comes up before then.

Suzanne left the meeting believing that Elizabeth's half of the problem had been solved. The conflict with Dave had not been resolved. Suzanne still needed to talk to him about his part. But she felt she had taken an assertive step in the right direction with her feuding employees.

~

Obviously, not all of your interactions with your employees will be about problems or negative situations. As a matter of fact, some potentially difficult events can bring out the best in others. For example, consider the surprising conversation Andrew S. (a thirty-year-old banking supervisor) had recently with one of his employees.

Case Study

During the first few weeks after Andy's promotion, a number of factors had started to affect the quality of his team's work. Because of limited resources, a high volume of work, and outdated equipment, Andy was having difficulty motivating a good group of employees. In fact, one or two people had simply resigned themselves to the fact (and told him) that things would never get better.

Many of Andy's employees had been in their positions for a long time and had become bored with some of the routine tasks. In fact, Andy had talked to them just the previous week about a sudden decline in the quality of their performance and their somewhat arrogant and abrasive approach to customers.

Then suddenly, one of Andy's veteran employees helped turn around this deteriorating situation. Susan M. assumed a leadership role with the team. She told Andy, in confidence, that she was sick and tired of the bad reputation the team was getting with customers and other departments. She told him that she could not change others, but that maybe her new attitude could help some of the younger employees. She then began to set a good example for everyone, including the handful of employees who seemed most cynical.

Andy was both surprised and pleased by her performance. Morale in his work area changed dramatically. So did productivity, quality, and response time. Customers commented, and department managers started giving Andy compliments about the excellent improvement they had noticed in his group. Andy could not wait to share the good news.

Analysis

Before you read about Andy's supervisory actions, take a few minutes to jot down some of your thoughts about this situation and how you would approach it.

_____

_____

_____

The Supervisor's Action

Because this was a significant development, Andy decided to take time at his regular staff meeting to recognize the whole team for its improvement and to acknowledge Susan for her outstanding contribution. He checked with her first to make sure she would not be overly embarrassed by a brief compliment, then he made these comments at the meeting:

If you've had a chance to review last month's closing figures, I'm sure you noticed the sharp increase in output and the lowest error rate we've had in over nineteen months. We've added two new customers, and at least three of our older customers have increased their purchases for next quarter. I know you've all been working hard, and I want you to know how much I personally appreciate your effort.

I would be remiss if I didn't single out one member of our team for her excellent individual performance during the past few weeks. I warned Susan that I wanted to give her some public recognition today, and she modestly said that what she's done is "no big deal." Well, I disagree, and I just want to say "Thanks, Susan" for an outstanding effort on our behalf. Your hard work has helped us turn around one of the worst downward swings I remember in all of my years with the company. Thanks for inspiring all of us.

Jim and other department managers are aware that our recent success did not come easily, that we are still struggling with limited resources and some outdated equipment. But the good news is that they have reopened lines of communication with some of our vendors about new computer systems and software. We're supposed to get an update about what's available early next month. Again, no promises, but I'm more optimistic than I was last month. Let me know if any of you have suggestions about what we need.

~

Let's look at one final awkward situation in which Bill S., a younger (twenty-nine years old) and less experienced manufacturing company supervisor, had to coach an older, veteran employee who wanted to put him in the middle with a supplier.

Case Study

George had worked in the purchasing department for almost twenty years. In fact, he had helped to start the department and had been a steady employee ever since. During his career, George had seen many changes in the industry and in the way his company did business. In recent conversations, Bill had realized that George had struggled with these changes. He had overcome an initial fear of computers and had learned to juggle an increasing number of reports and other new priorities. These adjustments had taken time, but Bill knew that George was pleased with his progress.

George's greatest strength had always been his relationship with vendors. He had known and worked with most of them for years. He was comfortable with them and was proud of the rapport he had established with them. Despite strong encouragement from Bill, however, George was having a difficult time telling one of these vendors, ABC Supplies, that its products and services were not meeting the company's current quality standards.

Bill believed that (objectively) George agreed with his assessment of ABC's quality. Bill also believed that (subjectively) George was having a very difficult time giving this "old friend" bad news. George had been doing business with this particular vendor for over fifteen years.

Analysis

Before reviewing Bill's supervisory actions, take a few minutes to write some of your thoughts about this situation. What would you do and why?

_____

_____

_____

The Supervisor's Action

After some initial encouragement, Bill convinced George to plan a course of action to resolve the problems with ABC Supplies. To show his support for George in this potentially embarrassing conversation, Bill offered to help George rehearse for the meeting. The supervisor started the meeting by stating:

George, I'm glad you've decided to talk with Mike Morro at ABC. I know you and Mike go way back, so I'm sure this conversation isn't going to be an easy one for you. I'm also glad you asked me to help you get ready for the meeting with Mike. Why don't we talk about some of the key issues you want to give him feedback about? In fact, would it help you if we practiced the conversation so that you can try out some of the exact words you want to use?

After the brief practice, Bill reinforced the positive elements of the planned meeting:

I liked the way you balanced your feedback to Mike. There were a few constructive suggestions, but there were also a number of sincere compliments. That should make the conversation easier for both of you. I think Mike will appreciate your honesty. I bet he thinks of you as an old friend, and I'm sure he wants to keep doing business with us. The tone of your whole conversation is, "How can we continue working together using our newest standards?" Mike should be able to make the necessary adjustments once he knows about them.

At the end of the meeting with George, Bill reiterated his willingness to support George's efforts and provided a final word of encouragement:

Why don't you stop by my office tomorrow after your meeting with Mike to let me know how things went? I'm sure you'll do a great job.

∼

As you probably have concluded from these brief case studies, there are several major factors that will usually affect the approach or supervisory style you use in particular situations. First of all, you will tend to do what you are most comfortable with, based on your own values, beliefs, experience, and feelings about the individual employee or employees. Second, you will consider the strengths, needs, interests, and level of competence of the people involved. You will factor in their willingness to assume responsibility, their need for direction or autonomy, their degree of interest in their work, and their level of commitment to company, department, and team objectives. Finally, you will evaluate the situation itself and determine the complexity, urgency, and importance of the work affected by the supervisory action you are planning to take. All of these situational factors will affect the approach you decide to use to supervise others.

Creating a Motivating Work Environment

First-line supervisors occasionally tell me about the successes they've had discussing expectations and work standards with their employees. They say it's almost like a light going on for both them and their direct reports. One person told me these conversations have helped her get a better understanding about what motivates the people she supervises, which has helped her make better decisions. Another supervisor told me he has improved his comfort level taking risks in certain situations. And one supervisor commented that these face-to-face meetings are so much more effective than communication by memo or voice-mail because he can raise issues, clarify concerns, and probe to find out a person's real feelings about a situation or assignment.

**—Michael F. McCarthy, personnel manager,
Rohm and Haas Company**

Once you have reviewed these case studies and thought about the style-preference questions earlier in this chapter, you should be prepared to discuss your expectations with your employees. In a way, this "clear the slate" meeting is your way of letting go of the past and setting a direction for the future. It is an important opportunity for all of you to discuss what will stay the same in the work environment and what will be different with you as their supervisor. The biggest challenge you face is creating the kind of environment that will be motivating for you and your employees.

Research shows that supervisors who use coercion, manipulation, and negative reinforcement will drive their employees to do mediocre work. This approach (motivation by coercion) creates short-term results delivered by employees who are intimidated and threatened to produce the minimum it takes to survive. "My way or the highway" is a shortsighted strategy that forces individuals to meet a supervisor's current demands—no more, no less—for as long as they can tolerate the pressure or until they can safely escape the oppressive situation.

On the other hand, supervisors who create a work environment in which people feel challenged, appreciated, and respected for their efforts will allow employees to drive themselves to do exceptional work. This approach (motivation by commitment) produces both excellent short-term results and valuable long-term contributions from individuals who feel supported, challenged, and encouraged to do their best by caring supervisors.

Studies comparing supportive and coercive work environments have determined that there are a number of things you can do to create an effective work climate, one in which your employees will commit themselves to doing exceptional work. These studies highlight how people work together in these positive, trusting atmospheres. Some of these techniques can be helpful to you when you are trying to establish or maintain a trusting work relationship with your employees:

- Be spontaneous and honest, rather than motivated by hidden agendas or ulterior motives. Deal with others honestly and without deception. Do not attempt to manipulate others or control them by imposing your personal attitudes on them.
- Understand the feelings of your employees, rather than appearing unconcerned or neutral about their welfare. Show empathy to reassure others that you can identify with their problems.
- When things go wrong, take a problem orientation rather than trying to control the situation or the person involved. A problem orientation implies a desire to collaborate in exploring a mutual problem. Try not to take

sides; be more interested in solving the problem than in assigning blame.

- Show respect for your employees by being open to new ideas. Value their contributions and build or maintain their self-esteem.
- Show a willingness to modify your own behavior and ideas whenever appropriate, rather than being rigid and narrow-minded. Remain open to new information. Do not give the impression that you know all the answers and do not need help from anyone.

Getting Commitment From Others

More and more, first line supervisors are being asked to provide business leadership, to identify the competencies required for future growth, and to foster collaboration among distinct, functional work units. More than ever before, supervisors have the opportunity and the responsibility to reinforce the behaviors required to sustain exceptional performance. The exciting and challenging part of their job is helping their teams align themselves with the values, standards, and best practices that will allow the organization to maintain a competitive position.

—Joseph Toto, director of organizational effectiveness, Hoffmann-LaRoche

When effective supervisors are asked to describe the secret of their success, many of them talk about their ability to encourage and sustain employee involvement. In some cases, these supervisors have redefined their job from "getting others to do what has to be done" to "getting others to *want* to do what has to be done."

As a supervisor, there are several other specific factors you can influence in order to maintain a healthy balance between motivation (personal incentives) and productivity (on-the-job performance) with your employees.

Understanding Expectations

Motivation and productivity are affected by a person's understanding of your expectations and acceptance of his or her job responsibilities. Problems can occur if there is a lack of understanding, a lack of agreement, or a lack of acceptance of current expectations and priorities. When these problems occur, here are two things you can do:

1. Maintain ongoing communication with your employees about expectations or priorities.
2. Discuss your reactions to changes that affect your job or your team's objectives first with your manager and then with your employees.

Personal Ability

Motivation and productivity are affected by your employees' ability to perform the tasks and meet the objectives that have been defined for them in their jobs. Some people are better than others at specific tasks. We all have different levels of knowledge, skill, and talent. Performance, therefore, will vary from person to person depending on how well individuals are able to do the work (competence) and how comfortable they are with their own ability (confidence). Problems can occur with your employees if they lack the knowledge or skill to perform the job, if they lack confidence in their ability to do the job required, or if a fear of failure, change, or some other unknown is affecting their productivity and morale. When these problems occur, here are some things you can do:

1. Initiate discussions with your employees about their developmental needs (knowledge/skills).
2. Maintain ongoing communication by providing regular feedback to your employees about their job performance.

3. Encourage your employees to discuss their concerns, frustrations, or needs.
4. Discuss your reactions to changes or new challenges that affect your employees' level of confidence and provide supportive coaching to help them through any tough spots.

Reward and Recognition

Motivation and productivity are affected by the rewards or benefits people get from doing a good job. Different individuals are motivated by different things. Some rewards are monetary and some are not. When people come to work each day, they are hoping that some of their needs (motivators) will be satisfied. Problems can occur with your employees if you misunderstand what motivates them, disagree about what motivates them, or are unwilling to meet their expectations, priorities, or needs. When these problems occur, here are some things you can do:

1. Take responsibility for initiating discussions with your employees so that you can clarify any confusion about what motivates them.
2. Maintain ongoing communication with your employees about their needs and primary motivators.
3. Encourage your employees to discuss their expectations, priorities, and needs.
4. To the best of your ability, respond to your employees' needs for reward and recognition.

Work Conditions

Motivation and productivity are affected by the conditions under which your employees perform their jobs. There are a number of important conditions that can affect their performance: safety, clear policies and procedures, resources, support from you and your manager, help from coworkers, proper equipment, and reputation (as a work group, department, or company). Problems can occur with your employees when there are sudden and unexpected changes in working conditions, a lack of support when changes occur (no advance communication or preparation time), and limited flexibility about priorities even though a change has occurred. When these problems arise, here are three things you can do:

1. Communicate openly with your employees about changing job conditions so that they understand why a different approach, direction, or priority is necessary.
2. Maintain ongoing problem-solving conversations with your employees about their frustrations, concerns, and difficulties dealing with the changes that have been made.
3. Encourage honest, ongoing self-assessments about how you and your employees need to change to meet the new job conditions and work requirements.

~

Years and volumes of research support the belief that a high level of involvement creates a greater sense of ownership and leads to dedicated commitment from employees. Most people do better work and enjoy it more when:

- They have a stake in the outcome.
- They feel personal pride and satisfaction in doing something that has value to themselves and others.
- They are given (or can take) credit for their efforts.
- They are encouraged to be the best they can be.

As a supervisor, your biggest challenge is to create the kind of work environment in which people feel good about themselves as often as possible. In other words, you will get consistently excellent performance from employees who believe they are valuable to you. You will not have to worry about how to motivate them. If you establish the right kind of climate, they will motivate themselves to do quality work.

Before moving on to Chapter 5, take a few minutes now to complete the following Journal Entry by highlighting some activities that have been motivating to you and might have a positive motivational effect on your employees.

Journal Entry   **Date:** _____

What can you do to create an environment that allows your employees to feel a sense of personal accomplishment? Some suggestions are listed below. Check off any that seem appropriate to your employees, then add any others that have helped you personally in the past.

- ☐ Encouragement (or at least permission) to voice their opinions about important work issues
- ☐ The opportunity to try new approaches and to question established ways of doing things
- ☐ A sense of control over their job and a feeling that they are accountable for their work habits and for quality results
- ☐ Regular and honest feedback from you, their supervisor, about how they are doing and how they can get better
- ☐ The right kinds of rewards at the right time for the right things

Others: _____

_____

Convert your ideas into a specific action plan by describing at least one thing you intend to do to improve or maintain your group's current work environment.

What will you do? _____

When? _____

5 | Setting Goals and Priorities

It is not enough to be busy. The question is: What are we busy about?

—Henry David Thoreau, American writer

In today's business world, we all have to make choices about how much time, money, or energy we can afford to spend on certain work activities. In the final analysis, your job performance and success will often be based on the quality of the decisions made at the start of a project or at the beginning of a work period.

Careful planning can ensure that you are allocating resources effectively: The most important tasks are getting done efficiently, and the least important tasks are getting only the minimum attention they deserve. You will be able to eliminate or deemphasize any tasks that are not contributing to your overall team or company objectives.

The thought process behind setting goals is often described as a "cascade" of critical information that answers these questions:

- What is my organization's purpose?
- What is my department's or team's purpose?
- What part does my team play in the organization?
- What do I and my team need to achieve?
- How will I know that I am effective and successful?

You and your manager can use this downward "funneling" technique to focus on specific team and individual objectives in a way that ensures that your work is connected to and aligned with broader, "big picture" corporate objectives. The following action steps can help you determine and manage priorities:

1. Review your company's mission statement and strategic objectives.
2. Review your department's mission statement and strategic objectives.
3. Develop your team's business goals by focusing on how you can contribute to organizational and departmental priorities.
4. Discuss with your manager how you think your team can make a contribution, and reach agreement about your short-term goals and priorities.
5. Communicate these goals and priorities to your team and anyone else who needs to know about them.
6. Periodically review your progress with your manager, your team members, and anyone else who needs to know.
7. Revise your goals and priorities when necessary to make sure your team is making a timely and meaningful contribution.
8. Demonstrate your commitment to important corporate or departmental initiatives and objectives.

Setting goals requires effective two-way communication so that important information flows upward, downward, and across the organization. Another way to look at alignment, therefore, is to ask a series of related *what/how/who* questions. The answers to these questions should produce a chain of related activities that will help you make certain you are contributing to important corporate objectives. Each of your major activities should state clearly:

- The goal for that activity (the "what")
- The work process, procedure, or technique (the "how") that delivers the result identified in the goal

- The measures to be used to evaluate progress and success
- The resources (the "who") needed to achieve the desired or required results

When you work with your manager to set individual and team objectives, you are working together to clarify key performance areas and to reach agreement about what you and your team are expected to accomplish during a defined time period. Objectives are mutually agreed-upon performance outcomes. Objectives help you understand what you have to do to ensure that your team's actions and priorities are in alignment with company goals. In *The Practice of Management,* Peter Drucker describes objectives as "the instrument panel necessary to pilot the business enterprise. Without them management flies by the seat of its pants—without landmarks to steer by, without maps and without having flown the route before."

It is smart for you to be sure that your objectives are summarized and written down. Writing them down will help you understand and remember them. Your written objectives then become a working document that you and your manager can use throughout the year for coaching, feedback, and progress reports. Your annual objectives are not intended to be your complete job description. They are the most important areas for you to focus on, and you should review, discuss, and revise them regularly.

Setting objectives with your manager will help you:

- Achieve your individual and team objectives.
- Ensure alignment with broader corporate objectives.
- Clarify expectations about duties, responsibilities, assignments, and priorities.
- Provide a method and system for coaching and performance-based feedback.
- Identify your individual strengths and interests.
- Keep your current job challenging and interesting.

When you and your manager write objectives, usually near the beginning of the year, you know that your objectives are likely to be aligned with corporate and departmental objectives.

When you and your manager revise objectives throughout the year, you know you are working on current priorities.

There are a number of critical outcomes that you are being paid to deliver. Discuss your current duties and responsibilities with your manager and anyone else who has influence over your job performance. Once you have defined the required or desired results, determine specific actions, techniques, and behaviors that will help you and your team deliver the expected outcomes. Your list may include special projects, temporary assignments, new priorities, or the routine activities you and your team engage in every day to meet your company's expectations and earn your paychecks. Above all, make sure you and your team are doing the right things right the first time.

As a new supervisor, you can use objectives to:

- Allocate resources.
- Give recognition for work well done.
- Review and adjust priorities to meet changes in the business.
- Establish a starting point for coaching and performance-based feedback.

Your employees can use objectives to:

- Understand what is expected of them.
- Track their own performance and progress.
- Control what they do and how they do it.

You need to understand what is expected of you so that your team's actions are aligned with company and departmental objectives. You share with your manager the responsibility for ensuring that the alignment is clear. High performance comes when you understand clearly what you have to do and when you can set challenging performance objectives for your team. The most frequent cause of poor performance is a lack of clarity about what is expected, not a lack of skills or a willingness to contribute. As Oliver Wendell Holmes once said, "The greatest thing in this world is not so much where we are, but in what direction we are moving."

Setting objectives is a continuous process in which you work together with your manager to identify key business processes; determine priorities, measures, and targets; define cross-functional or team objectives; and clarify individual, personal goals for the year. For Tony Barth, goal setting includes planning: "Goal setting is the forum that provides context and identifies for people their *sphere of influence*. Goal setting clarifies role contributions, impact, and key areas of responsibility."

The process should allow for flexibility and adaptability; it should be based on real work that encourages commitment and accountability. Many people have found the mnemonic SMART helpful in developing and discussing good objectives:

S pecific
M easurable
A chievable
R elevant
T ime-Bound

A performance requirement is *specific* if it states what is to be done and describes behaviors that can be seen as leading to the attainment of the objective. The activities necessary to achieve the goal need not be listed or discussed unless you find doing so useful or necessary.

A goal should be *measurable*. How well something is done might reflect its timeliness, accuracy, cost, and completeness. While some jobs lend themselves more easily to quantitative analysis, all objectives should be framed in such a way that you can determine reasonably whether and to what extent they have been reached. There are two different types of measurements:

1. *Results measures* tell you and others what work is getting done. They are used to monitor the outputs of the work process so that these outputs meet customer or company requirements. These measures focus on outcomes, deliverables, or accomplishments such as total sales, on-time shipments, or number of new products. They give you hard data about your team's output and its delivery of desired or required results.

2. *Process measures* indicate how work is getting done. They are used to ensure that you and your team are doing what has to be done to achieve the desired outcomes. To develop process

measures, you first identify the desired result and then define what needs to be done to reach this result.

Results measures show *whether* your team is actually giving the organization and your customers what they want. Process measures show *how* your processes are working to give the organization and your customers what they want. Monitor and measure your progress and accomplishments. Use established benchmarks, target dates, or schedules to determine how well you and your team are moving toward accomplishing your desired goals.

An objective must not be unreachable or beyond what could reasonably be expected. Performance requirements should be *achievable*, but they should also challenge you and your team. They should encourage your team to give the most of its talent, ability, and energy. You should feel comfortable discussing with your manager whether you have the authority, resources, and capability to achieve a particular objective.

All performance objectives should be *relevant*—selected because they support the mission, purpose, and strategy of the organization and the particular division or unit within the organization. Ideally, you should review your objectives with your manager after department objectives have cascaded down from higher levels in the company. You should also have a clear idea about your priorities.

An objective should be *time-bound*—an activity, task, or process that must be completed by a particular date, on a regular schedule, or on a routine basis. You should know when or how often specific tasks need to be completed.

Finally, objectives should be discussed and documented so that you can receive, understand, and act on feedback about the results of your individual performance. A self-monitoring system allows for ongoing evaluation, improvement, and development. You and your manager share responsibility for maintaining alignment and achieving success. SMART objectives set the stage for future conversations. Try using the following checklist to help you double-check the quality of your current goals.

☐ Does the goal statement describe a key result and a target date?

☐ Is the goal measurable and verifiable, and do I have responsibility for final results?

☐ Does the goal relate to one of my key job responsibilities? Is the goal truly significant or merely routine?

☐ Does the goal relate to one of my company's functional
objectives or current strategies?

☐ Can the goal be understood by others involved in implementation?

☐ Is the goal realistic and attainable, but also challenging?

☐ Will the result, when achieved, justify the effort required to achieve it? Is there a cost-to-benefit payoff?

☐ Is the goal consistent with current policies and procedures?

☐ Can various performance stages or levels of accomplishment be clearly distinguished to facilitate evaluation of
results?

Once you and your manager have defined all of your objectives, here are some questions to help you prioritize them:

1. Of all the objectives you have written, which ones are
   most valuable or significant to your team?
2. Which are most supportive of your company's mission,
   purpose, and strategic objectives?
3. If you could accomplish only three or four of your objectives, which ones would you work on?
4. Which of your objectives will yield the highest payoff,
   first to your company and then to you?
5. What will happen if you do not achieve these objectives? What will be the negative consequences for you
   and for your company?
6. Will failure to achieve any one of these goals cause you
   to get fired, demoted, transferred, or held back from future promotions?

Goals and objectives will help you move forward in a certain direction. But not every goal should be pursued at the same
speed. Once you have established a goal, you need to place a
value on it. The value should be based primarily on what must
be done, not on what you or your team prefer to do or enjoy

doing. Once you have placed a value on the goal, you have established its priority. Make sure that what you think is important is consistent with what others in the organization need from your team.

This prioritizing process requires an honest analysis of your team's current assignments, methods, and preferences. Are you doing certain things out of habit or tradition only? Do you spend too much time doing the things you like at the risk of shortchanging more important, less enjoyable tasks? Are you letting significant work go until tomorrow or trying to catch up with it during nonbusiness hours?

Questions of priority usually involve two factors: *importance* and *urgency*. You are trying to determine if the right tasks are getting appropriate attention to meet required budget and time guidelines. Although you may need to change the wording to reflect your own situation, the chart below provides a simple formula for determining priorities:

Importance	Urgency
The effect this task will have on personal or team accomplishments:	When the project, task, or activity must be completed to meet required deadlines:
5 = Critical	5 = This month
4 = Necessary	4 = Next month
3 = Important	3 = This quarter
2 = Helpful	2 = Next quarter
1 = Marginal	1 = End of the year

Importance × Urgency = Priority
A = 16–25
B = 9–15
C = 1–8

This formula can help you pick the right words when you are discussing priorities with others. For example, an "A" priority might be something that is "critical for us to finish by the end of next month" and a "B" priority might be something that is "important for us to finish by the end of this quarter."

The following questions can help you confirm the priority you have assigned specific goals so that you can be sure you are emphasizing the right things for you and your team:

1. Is this a priority that you have attained or tried to attain in the past?
2. If yes, did you attain it with ease? with challenge? with great difficulty?
3. If you attempted but did not attain it, why not?

   - Priority set too high
   - Not enough resources
   - Not enough skill
   - Extenuating circumstances

4. If there have been extenuating circumstances in the past, have the circumstances been corrected?
5. Have you prioritized this goal differently in the past? Higher? Lower?
6. Does the goal or priority contribute directly to your company's current priorities?
7. Does the prioritizing of your goal reflect its importance as a company or departmental goal?
8. If this goal or priority were met, what would be the impact on:

   - Your professional development?
   - Your relationship with your team?
   - Departmental or functional goals or priorities?
   - Corporate goals or priorities?

9. If this goal or priority were *not* met, what would be the impact on:

   - Your professional development?
   - Your relationship with your team?
   - Departmental or functional goals or priorities?
   - Corporate goals or priorities?

10. Does this goal or priority contribute to the long-term

growth of your company? Will it be important three to five years from now?

There are several additional steps you can take to clarify and communicate priorities:

1. Meet with your manager to discuss long-range objectives and short-range strategies or projects that support these broader goals. Review your understanding of priorities from earlier meetings about these topics.

2. Translate these unit goals into individual performance objectives for your employees, remembering their current job responsibilities, talents, and interests. Try to identify tasks that need to be clarified, reinforced, or delegated.

3. Anticipate problems and develop contingency plans that will reduce the likelihood of a problem's occurring (the cause) or that will minimize the impact if the problem does occur (the effects). For instance, if problems occur, you may want to establish a standard for more frequent meetings to discuss and communicate priorities.

4. Discuss your operational plans with your employees in a group (for team projects) and in private (for individual assignments). Remember the importance of participation and active involvement in this goal-setting process. Ask for suggestions, reactions, or concerns about what you are asking your employees to do, how they will meet their goals, and how you/they will measure their performance.

These meetings will establish performance guidelines and evaluation criteria for the course of a specific project or for the duration of a particular appraisal period (usually one year). The more attention you give to these details now, the easier your employees' job will be in meeting your expectations and the easier your job will be in evaluating their accomplishments fairly. Here are some suggestions to make this stage of the process go smoothly for you:

1. Use realistic time projections, including accurate and adequate room for error.

2. When possible, use quantitative evaluation criteria, such as number of items processed, projects completed, time and cost factors, number of complaints received or resolved, or any other objective and tangible measurement of work output or results.

3. Discuss qualitative evaluation criteria as well, giving special attention to important behavioral components of the job, such as safety, quality, interpersonal effectiveness, teamwork, initiative or creativity, adherence to company policies, or any other subjective measurements related to how results should be achieved.

Remember, whatever you are trying to achieve, you cannot do it alone. Ultimately, you are responsible for what *you* accomplish and the actions *you* take every minute of every day. But this takes teamwork, getting commitments from others, integrating your plans and actions with those of others. Once you have a clear action plan, therefore, it is important that you decide who will affect your plan and who will be affected by it. Ask yourself:

- Who needs to know my goals and priorities?
- Why do they need to know? Can they help me achieve success or could they interfere with my team's progress?
- How would I like them to collaborate with me?
- What information or help do I need from them?
- When will I need their help?
- What contingencies should I consider and discuss with them?

It is important that you anticipate problems. Incorporate into your strategic thinking both contingency planning and risk analysis. Do not dwell too long on negative possibilities, but be proactive about problems that can be avoided, managed, or minimized. Be specific about what you need from others. Then set realistic deadlines based on when you need their help and when they will be able to give it. Sometimes your best-laid plans fail because you have underestimated or forgotten the impact that others can have on your activities.

Planning to Succeed

A plan outlines what is to be done and the order in which steps must be taken to reach a final goal. A good plan can be an effective road map that lets you and your team know:

- When to get started on certain tasks
- How much time, money, and energy you can afford to spend on specific activities
- Which deadlines need to be met in order for you to reach your final destination on schedule

Planning and organizing your group's work usually involves the following action steps:

1. Study the situation and select a general method or approach to meet a goal or solve a problem.
2. Gain agreement and support from others who will influence, implement, or be affected by your plan.
3. Develop your plan by defining:

   - Specific tasks and activities
   - Resources required (including people, time, money, materials)
   - Sequential and concurrent activities
   - Time allocations and a schedule

4. Test and review your plan with others both within and outside your group.
5. Implement your plan and revise it to meet any unexpected contingencies.
6. Follow up on a regular basis with those involved in (or affected by) your plan.

Case Study

As a result of his team's recent success on a similar engineering project, Mark's work group was given responsibility for developing a prototype of a new water-purification device known simply as "Model Jupiter." Last Friday, Mark's manager came to one of Mark's regular staff meetings and discussed some of the available design specifications for the new product. He also reviewed current budget constraints ($1.5 million) and described some of the marketing advantages of having this new device available by the end of the third quarter. He admitted that the design schedule was extremely tight—the first prototype was to be available for marketing within six months, or by August 15 at the latest. He then encouraged Mark and his team to develop an action plan that would include both individual and team objectives. Mark agreed to meet with the five members of his project team and report back to his manager within two weeks.

Analysis

Before you read about Mark's supervisory actions, take a few minutes to jot down some of your thoughts about this goal-setting opportunity and how you would handle it.

_____

_____

_____

The Supervisor's Action

Mark began his planning meeting with his project team by discussing an overall objective written according to SMART guidelines:

> Develop a prototype of Model Jupiter for marketing by August 15 that meets all design specifications and budget requirements outlined at last week's staff meeting and documented in minutes of the senior management meeting dated January 4.

From that broad perspective, Mark and his team began developing specific goals and action steps that would get the results they needed by the required date. In fact, they described a dozen action items and then went on to assign individual responsibility and target dates for each item. As their plan took shape, they clarified the key results they needed to achieve at each step and defined checkpoints where they could measure progress and interim accomplishments. For example, the action steps they listed included the following four items:

Step 1: Mark and John will meet with production managers by January 15 to understand their current-year production schedules and priorities.

Step 3: Frank and Mary will meet with marketing managers by February 25 to discuss their customers' expectations of the new product and to compare customers' needs with the available design specifications.

Step 6: Mark, Mary, and John will demonstrate the new product at a senior management meeting on April 10. The purpose of the meeting will be to identify potential "bugs" that need to be addressed before the team makes a preliminary presentation to preferred customers on May 25.

Step 9: Begin production of the new prototype on June 6 for initial distribution on July 30.

A project plan and specific goals like those determined by Mark and his team can set the stage for ongoing coaching and feedback so that team members know how they are doing and what they may need to do to improve.

Communicate Your Expectations Clearly

A team needs a common purpose that is understood, shared, and felt to be worthwhile by its members (sometimes described as a mission, mandate, or objective). Teams need to know why they exist, what they are supposed to accomplish, and how they are to coordinate with other groups to reach their goals. Your team members expect you to know the direction they are to take and to set a course of action that will lead them to individual and collective success. As Yogi Berra once said, "If you don't know where you are going, you might wind up someplace else." Your team members will expect you to:

- Interpret goals passed down from higher levels.
- Translate current organizational needs into team goals and objectives.
- Develop strategies and action plans that will lead to successful results.
- Identify resources (people, time, money, materials, and facilities) needed to achieve desired results.
- Establish time lines, schedules, and completion dates.
- Determine standards of performance for the team and for individual team members.

The ultimate test of a team is its ability to achieve results that the individual team members cannot achieve by themselves. The team's diverse talents combine to create an end product that is beyond the team members' individual capability. In general, there are several supervisory actions that can help you communicate and manage priorities effectively:

1. Be accessible. Review objectives, expectations, and progress frequently.
2. Give honest, accurate, and timely feedback regularly.
3. Provide positive and supportive coaching whenever appropriate. Provide constructive and helpful criticism whenever necessary.
4. Arrange for support, including training or on-the-job coaching. Negotiate for resources (time, money, equipment).
5. Know what motivates individuals. Match appropriate challenges to individual interests and needs.
6. Make sure good performance is not punished. For example, when someone does a good job on a project, there is a tendency to assign that person several other projects. Good performers, therefore, may be "rewarded" by having additional work dumped on them.
7. Make sure poor performance is not rewarded. For example, failure to confront someone whose performance is not meeting expectations can create an impression that poor performance is tolerated, ignored, or accepted.

Trying to get your employees to do an unreasonable amount of work can backfire. To be effective, performance goals and objectives have to be within the range of what an average person can achieve. If work goals are unrealistic, you can create dissatisfaction and damage morale. People will feel overwhelmed and frustrated.

However, many people do not work at full efficiency, and some experts believe that it is usually possible for the average employee to produce about 10 percent more than he or she actually produces. If you believe that a 10 percent improvement is possible and reasonable, ask your employees for that modest increase. Most employees will try to do what is reasonable. There is also some satisfaction associated with accomplishing a slightly higher goal—although the thrill will wear off quickly if you repeatedly ask for more output.

When employees achieve the extra work you requested, be sure to recognize and acknowledge the improvement. Sometimes a simple "thank you" is all you need: "Mary, that was good work. Thanks for improving your efforts last week." Another way to express your appreciation is to show your enthusiasm for the improvement: "Lee, congratulations on the new production rate. Let's see if we can keep things at this level. It would be great for the whole team to follow your example."

In order to determine and communicate clear objectives and priorities, you must dedicate time for planning. Use this time to:

- Clarify long-range objectives and monthly goals.
- Write out daily and weekly plans with priorities and deadlines.
- Anticipate problems and develop contingency plans.
- Use realistic time projections, including accurate and adequate room for error.
- Anticipate when crunches might occur so that you can communicate what's going on with your team to those who need to know.
- Discuss your plans and priorities with others who will affect them or be affected by them.

Finally, spend some time on contingency planning by determining what could possibly go wrong with your plans. Consider some of the following potential problems that could affect you and your team's performance:

- Equipment problems
- Inaccurate time estimates
- Materials arriving late
- Substandard inventory
- Inexperienced employees
- Operational changes
- Increased workload
- Conflicting priorities
- Absenteeism
- Interpersonal disagreements

Then formalize a contingency plan by taking the following actions:

1. Define the contingencies by stating what is most likely to go wrong and how much risk is involved.
2. Work with your team to develop a plan to handle those contingencies. Either address the *causes* of a problem (to minimize the likelihood of its occurring) or address the *effects* of a problem (to minimize the impact if it does occur).
3. Implement and monitor the whole plan, then communicate what you are doing to your manager and others who need to know.

Before moving on to Chapter 6, take a few minutes now to practice writing and prioritizing your current goals. Then decide what personal obstacles might get in your way and determine how you will deal with these potential barriers.

Journal Entry **Date:** _____

1. Take a few minutes now to practice writing one of your most important objectives using the SMART guidelines.

Writing Objectives Using SMART Guidelines

Specific—What am I trying to produce or accomplish and how?
_____

_____

Measurable—How will I know that I have accomplished the objective or that I am moving in the right direction? _____

_____

Achievable—What resources and authority do I need? _____

_____

Relevant—How will this objective affect company or department
activities? _____

_____

Time-Bound—When or how often does this objective need to be
accomplished? _____

_____

---

2. Now, take a few minutes to write down your team's three most important goals or objectives.

_____

_____

_____

3. Finally, take a few minutes to develop a brief contingency plan for yourself, describing how you will deal with any of the following time wasters. What will you need to deal with to ensure that you are able to communicate and accomplish your team goals?

- Lack of planning
- Unclear priorities or objectives
- Poor communication
- Unrealistic expectations
- Doing what should be delegated
- Meetings
- Any other contingency you need to address

_____

_____

_____

6 | Communication

You can have brilliant ideas, but if you can't get them across, your ideas won't get you anywhere.

—Lee Iacocca, former chairman, Chrysler Corporation

Most effective supervisors say that communication skills are essential to their success. Experts define communication as the process of creating "common understanding" by sharing ideas, facts, and feelings. Some of the important goals of communication include being understood, teaching or instructing someone else, gaining acceptance or agreement, understanding how others feel or what they have to say, and getting something done. When communication works well, information is transmitted as successfully as possible from sender to receiver. It is then processed, reviewed, clarified, and revised until both sender and receiver completely understand each other. The challenge for you in all of your interactions with others is to overcome some of the common barriers to effective communication:

- Noises and other physical conditions in the environment that make hearing difficult
- Fatigue, hunger, or other physiological obstacles
- The emotional state and feelings of both the sender and the receiver (anger, confidence, fear)
- The importance of the topic or the agenda
- Inappropriate or confusing nonverbal or body language
- The time, timing, place, and structure of the meeting
- Personal attitudes, including stereotypes, biases, and prejudicial opinions
- Interruptions and distractions

- Vocabulary or terminology that creates misunderstanding or is subject to misinterpretation
- Conflicting intentions on the part of the people who are trying to communicate that can lead to rejection, disagreement, and uncertainty

Effective communication is a two-way process that requires skill in both receiving and giving information. Because the focus so far in this book has been mostly on understanding what others expect of you, start by reviewing several communication techniques that can help you when you are requesting and receiving information and opinions from others:

1. Demonstrate that you are receptive to the information you have requested. Listen patiently to what the other person is saying, even if you believe it is wrong or irrelevant. Indicate simple acceptance (not necessarily agreement) by nodding or injecting an occasional "um-hm" or "I see." Concentrate on the speaker's message. Stay focused.

2. Show interest. Listen carefully and attentively. Try to understand both the content of the message and the other person's feelings about the message. Most people have difficulty talking clearly about their feelings, so paying careful attention is necessary. Listen also for what is *not* said—avoiding key points or agreeing too quickly may be clues to something the person really wants to discuss. Body language, eye contact, tone of voice, and other cues might be part of the message being sent.

3. Ask questions to make sure you understand. Ask clarifying questions if you are not clear about the meaning of the message. Ask probing questions to learn more about the content or context of the message.

4. Paraphrase or restate to make sure you have interpreted the information correctly. Confirm what you have heard by repeating or clarifying words, meanings, and feelings.

5. Allow time for the discussion to continue without interruption. Focus on the content of the message. There is a saying that most people, when they are having conversations with

others, spend their time either talking or waiting to talk. Listening is often overlooked as an important communication skill, and it is often viewed as a passive activity rather than an active opportunity to collect important information. Work on making yourself an effective listener by consciously committing your time and energy to paying attention to what the other person has to say.

6. Try not to spend your listening time thinking about your next response. Reserve your evaluation of the other person's message until you are certain you understand that message clearly. Interrupt only to clarify what the other person is saying or feeling.

7. Do not make judgments until you have received all the information, then respond to the message you have received in a way that shows you have listened carefully. If the person genuinely wants your viewpoint, be honest in your response. But in the listening process, try to limit expressing your views, since these may affect how the other person responds. Remember that what you should be most interested in is the other person's honest opinions, not a reflection of your own views.

8. Reach agreement about what the other person's feedback means to you and to her or him. Remember that willingness to listen is one of the hallmarks of trusting communication.

When you need to request information, determine the most effective way to get the results you want by asking yourself a series of focused questions: What do I need to know, and who has the information I need? What is the best (fastest, clearest, easiest) way for me to get the information I need? When and why do I need the information?

When you need to receive information, prepare for your conversation by asking yourself several additional questions: What do I need to do to ensure that I get timely, accurate, and complete information from others? How do I let others know that they can give me the information I need even if it is bad news or difficult feedback? What steps do I need to take to strengthen my interpersonal relationships with the key people I depend on for information?

The other important component of effective communication, giving information and feedback to others, is a way of helping them understand your preferences, values, and expectations. You are now in a position that requires you to discuss with your employees your reactions to their performance and work habits. It will be important for you to give your employees honest, timely, accurate, and objective feedback. You will need to be tactful and sensitive in your approach, but it will be critical to your success and theirs that you share information that they need to improve their work and their relationship with you.

Later in the book, you will have an opportunity to take a closer look at giving constructive feedback to your employees in situations in which there are serious or recurring problems. For now, however, there are several key skills for you to begin practicing whenever you are giving information or feedback to others:

1. Test to see if the other person is receptive to your feedback. Select the best time, place, and approach. Use the right style, words, and tone.
2. Be specific and clear. Focus on behavior (not the person), the specific (not generalizations), descriptions (not value judgments), and the person's immediate short-term need for feedback or information.
3. Check to make sure the other person understands your feedback. Make sure the other person is not reading something into your message, listening selectively, or hearing a different message from the one you are sending.
4. Validate your feedback by using examples and other supporting information. Repeat the critical details to be sure your message has been received accurately. Summarize your feedback and ask for agreement about the message you have sent.

When you need to *give* information to others, ask yourself focused questions about the most effective way to get the results you want: What do I need to do to ensure that my communication is timely, accurate, and complete? What facts or examples can I use to ensure that my communication is data-based and objective? What is the best way—time, place, method—for me to give information to people above me in the organization?

Certain situations may also require different approaches. The way you communicate with your manager is probably different from the way you communicate with peers, customers, suppliers, or any other key people you interact with on a regular basis. You may also find that communicating with your employees will be different at different times. You will need to decide when one-on-one communication is better than bringing the whole team together. You may also find that certain individuals need to receive information in greater detail than others. Another employee may want to know why your conversation is important or necessary. In these situations you will need to determine the most effective way to get your message across clearly and concisely.

Effective communication is *primarily* the speaker's responsibility. When you are sending a message to someone else, be sure it is sent in an open, honest, and clear manner so that it does not require a great deal of decoding by the receiver. You need to be alert for any signs that the receiver may be confused or may be having difficulty understanding your message. You need to be aware of the nonverbal aspects of communication (body language, gestures, eye contact, appearance, intonation, and facial expressions) to ensure that no mixed messages are being sent.

Finally, effective communication depends largely on your reputation, credibility, and intention. When you are the speaker, the person sending a message to someone else, the success of your communication will depend on how the other person answers these questions about you:

- Have you been clear, straightforward, honest, and trustworthy in the past?
- Can the person you are talking with believe you and your message?
- Does the other person believe that the conversation is an attempt to manipulate, embarrass, or dominate him or her?

- Can the other person trust your motives, or is there a possibility that you have a hidden agenda?

Mastering good communication skills is so vital to your success as a supervisor that you will have many additional opportunities throughout this book to develop and practice these skills. Almost every chapter will emphasize some type of communication activity or application. Along with decision making and problem solving, communication is one of the three foundation blocks of successful supervision.

In the following case studies, notice how the supervisors use effective communication skills to get immediate results and establish rapport with their employees. Paul's approach is firm and focused; Dana's approach is supportive and helpful.

Case Study

On Friday afternoon, Paul left instructions that specific analyses were to be completed over the weekend by the shift technician, Dan. Paul estimated that these analyses would take two or three hours of Dan's time.

On Monday, Paul discovered that Dan had not done the analyses. Since there were no apparent problems in the plant over the weekend, Paul wanted to meet with Dan to see if there was a logical explanation for not completing the work. Dan had had problems in the past completing work on time and doing work assignments in the order of priority that Paul had established for him. In the past, Dan had used a number of excuses like:

I didn't realize that the analyses were that important.

I got busy with other things.

I was helping another technician with a problem.

There's so much to do that certain things have to be let go until another time.

Paul suspected that Dan just hated doing these analyses, and that he intentionally left them for someone else. When Paul decided to discuss this situation, he realized that he needed to start by getting some additional information from Dan.

Analysis

Before you read how Paul handled this situation, take a few minutes to jot down what you would do, what you would say, and what you would like Dan to do as a result of your meeting.

The Supervisor's Action

When confronted with this situation, Paul started by giving Dan direct feedback about the problem. He began by stating the facts:

I assigned the analyses to you as part of your weekend work schedule. There were no unusual incidents that would have kept you from completing this assignment. What happened?

The open-ended question gave Dan an opportunity to begin listing some of his customary excuses. Paul listened and asked clarifying questions:

What were the two or three most time-consuming activities that pulled you away from these analyses?

You said you were helping another technician. Exactly how long did this take?

What do I need to do in the future to convince you that these analyses are an important part of your job?

After hearing Dan's responses, Paul asked Dan whether he had actually even started the analyses. He learned that Dan had done some preliminary work but still had close to two hours of work left. Paul then moved on to developing and discussing an action plan with Dan:

> It would be unfair to the other technicians for me to ask them to complete your work. I needed these analyses today, but I'll ask for an extension on my deadline until late Wednesday. That will give you a few days to work this assignment into your schedule. Sometime between now and then I expect you to complete these analyses according to our current standards. Why don't you tell me what you can do to get this job done by then?

Dan decided to work through his breaks on Monday and to cut a few minutes from his lunch time. He agreed to give Paul a brief status report at the end of the day so that they could both decide whether Dan needed to come in early or stay late on Tuesday to get the assignment under control. Paul ended by reinforcing the importance of this task:

> Very few people enjoy doing these analyses, Dan. They are a necessary but bothersome part of our work. However, you must be willing to share the work fairly with others. So it is not important that you like this task, but it is important that you do it effectively and on time. I need to continue assigning these analyses to you on certain weekends, and I need to be able to count on you to get them done without additional reminders or prodding from me. Can you agree that this will not happen again?

Paul's conversation was a successful combination of getting and giving both information and feedback. There was an honest exchange in which Paul stayed focused on two desired outcomes: getting Dan to complete the analyses and helping him to understand that they are an important part of his job.

Case Study

Dwight had been a team leader for almost a year. During the past few months, Dana had been scheduled to attend several off-site meetings, and she needed to depend on Dwight to take care of a few things while she was gone. There were several monthly reports that he needed to complete and a number of other administrative details that she wanted to review with him before she left. Dana wanted to emphasize the importance of these tasks so that Dwight did not put them off until she got back. Dana realized that this would be a good time to emphasize that Dwight needed to continue shifting his technical work to someone else so that he would have more time for these administrative responsibilities.

Analysis

Before you read how Dana handled this situation, take a few minutes to jot down what you would do, what you would say, and what you would like Dwight to do as a result of your meeting.

_____

_____

_____

The Supervisor's Action

Dana approached this situation as an opportunity to reinforce her earlier delegation conversation with Dwight. The meeting focused on defining specific team-leader responsibilities (monthly reports and administrative details like time sheets and vacation schedules) and then moved on to an open-ended discussion about Dwight's comfort level with the new job. Dana asked several open-ended questions to help her get the information she needed:

How are things going with the team?

How are you feeling about your current projects?

What technical tasks are taking up your time and creating crunches for you with your project team responsibilities?

What help do you need from me before I leave for New York?

Dana and Dwight talked about several things Dwight needed to help build his confidence concerning his new job. They discussed the skill levels of two team members who might be able to take on some of Dwight's current technical tasks, and Dana agreed to help Dwight prepare for conversations with them when she returned from her trip. Finally, Dana encouraged Dwight to be patient with the new job and reinforced her confidence in him as a person she trusted to make the transition smoothly and effectively. She ended the meeting with one last offer of help—"What else can I do?"—to which Dwight responded, "Leave me telephone numbers so I can get in touch with you if I need to." The comfortable exchange of information helped both supervisor and employee clarify current expectations and strengthen their interpersonal relationship.

Communication and Teamwork

Good teamwork depends on good communication. Peter Drucker once said that 60 percent of the problems in the workplace are the result of faulty communication. To be an effective team leader, therefore, you need to sharpen your basic communication skills so that you are able to use them to your best advantage in both individual and group interactions. Often the challenge is to balance your need to produce results with your need to build and maintain comfortable working relationships. Communication skills can help you accomplish both of these desired outcomes with your team.

Effective supervisors manage to focus appropriate attention on both task accomplishment (*what* gets done) and team relationships (*how* the task gets done). This allows the team not only to achieve success, but also to share a sense of accomplishment about what it has taken to succeed. There are a variety of specific roles and behaviors associated with the way team members interact with one another to accomplish their purpose. As team leader, when you and your team are focused on task accomplishment, there are several specific communication techniques you can use and encourage others to emulate. For example, you can:

- Initiate action by proposing a task, defining a problem, suggesting a solution, or recommending an idea or a procedure.
- Request information by asking for suggestions or ideas, seeking data or examples, or requesting confirmation or clarification.
- Give information by offering suggestions or ideas, presenting data or examples, or providing confirmation or clarification.
- Test progress by making critical assessments of new ideas or recommendations, evaluating team productivity or efficiency; or reminding the team of deadlines, budgets, and commitments.
- Summarize by restating ideas or conclusions after team discussions, paraphrasing a decision for the team to accept or reject, or pulling together related ideas for the team to review.

As a team leader, when you and your team are focused on interpersonal relationships, you may decide to use some of the following communication techniques. You can look for opportunities to:

- Encourage others to participate.
- Recognize others for their contributions.
- Open up discussions so that others feel comfortable contributing their ideas.
- Ask for opinions, feelings, and suggestions so that others know their ideas are valued.
- Suggest procedures for dealing with team problems, conflicts, or decisions.
- Clarify ideas or suggestions, help clear up any confusion, and seek consensus.
- Reduce tension by encouraging harmony or by helping to make an objective evaluation of interpersonal differences.
- Suggest workable compromises in the best interest of the team.

- Collaborate with others and set an example of how people can work together.
- Build productive relationships with your team members and encourage them to do the same with you and with one another.

Team goals and outcomes are achieved through mutual trust, respect, and support. Very little that is worth much is accomplished by getting what you want at someone else's expense. If you are perceived as trustworthy, others will feel comfortable expressing their ideas, feelings, disagreement, and opinions. If you are perceived as untrustworthy, others will withhold important information, values, and perspectives that could be valuable input for you and others on your team. Giving people encouragement and positive feedback goes a long way toward establishing a productive and comfortable work environment for everyone. Offering your employees information, strategies, support, and solutions that will be mutually beneficial can help establish long-lasting relationships that will make life more productive for everyone.

Effective supervisors know how to get what they want without hurting themselves or others. They have identified their interpersonal strengths and continue to capitalize on them. Here are a few communication strategies that effective supervisors use that can help you become more effective in your leadership position:

1. *Share information with others who will benefit from knowing what you know.* If you are not certain whether a piece of information is important to your employees, let them decide—"I heard something about your project that I thought you might like to know," or "Would you be interested in this magazine article I read recently about our new computer software?" Offers like this can help establish your reputation as someone who keeps in touch with people about their interests or needs and is willing to pass along data that can be useful to them.

2. *Compliment others for their efforts and good work.* Be sincere and factual. Sometimes a simple, "Thank you for getting that information to me so quickly" can make an employee feel val-

ued. Stating your appreciation or noticing someone's contribution shows that you are interested in that person's work and your relationship with him or her. Often, in the rush of our daily lives, we forget to pass on an encouraging word to someone who could use a lift or a positive remark. Sometimes asking an employee's advice can be a nice way to compliment that employee on her or his expertise or performance—"I know you have made several successful presentations recently, and I was wondering whether you took questions during your presentation or asked people to wait until the end?" or "Congratulations on meeting that deadline. How did you do it?" Giving employees an opportunity to brag a little about their good work reinforces your interest in working together in a cooperative atmosphere. You and your team members are working together toward a common goal, and opportunities to support each other should not be minimized or ignored. A few positive comments can help others keep their problems in perspective. You can maintain the spirit of cooperation that is an important characteristic of all successful teams.

3. *In your efforts to streamline work processes and keep things moving smoothly from your work area to the next, remember the importance of communicating with your peers and your manager.* If you see a potential problem or actual bottleneck, do your best to remove any obstacles that may adversely affect your team's efforts, and keep others informed about any pending delays or other problems. If your team's part of the work is slowing down or going off track, communicate with anyone who needs to know. Do not hesitate to ask for suggestions or resources from employees who might have a better perspective on ways to improve their work.

4. *Offer your opinions and give employees useful, data-based information that will help them maintain or improve their current performance.* Coaching requires sensitivity to the feelings of team members. Careful, thoughtful preparation can help you present your views in a way that the receiver will find beneficial. The employee must understand, accept, and be able to act on your feedback. To make this process work, try to use specific details and examples, talk to people when they are most receptive to

hearing from you, allow adequate time to discuss your feed-back, and reach agreement about the purpose and content of your message.

Giving and getting feedback can improve teamwork. Shar-ing your perceptions about your employees' performance and work habits is the only way you can help them modify their actions, achieve better results, or continue doing something they are currently doing well. Remember, the purpose of any performance-based feedback is to encourage someone to start doing something new, continue doing something that he or she is doing well, or stop doing something that is ineffective or in-appropriate. If you are tactful and diplomatic, you can keep even your most critical observations constructive and ensure that your honest feedback is appreciated and used. Regardless of the specific topic of conversation—whether you are setting goals, delegating tasks, analyzing problems, or making deci-sions—your communication skills can make the difference for both you and your team.

Before moving on to Chapter 7, take a few minutes to com-plete the following Journal Entry by reviewing specific situa-tions that will require you to receive and give information or feedback. Focus also on those communication skills that you want to remember to use or to develop in these supervisory situations.

Journal Entry   **Date:** _____

The Value of Requesting Information or Feedback

1. As a supervisor, there are times when you cannot afford to be in the dark about what's going on in your work areas. List at least two specific situations or occasions when it will be critical for you to request information from your manager, your employees, or a peer in your own or another department.

   _____

   _____

2. There are also occasions when it is important for employees to know that you value their perceptions, opinions, and ideas. List at least two specific situations or occasions when employees may want you to make a special effort to request information or feedback from them.

   _____

   _____

3. What skills or techniques will you focus on when you are requesting information or feedback from others?

   _____

   _____

The Value of Giving Information or Feedback

1. As a supervisor, there are time when you cannot afford to withhold information, to keep others in the dark, or to allow others to have blind spots that go unnoticed. List at least two specific situations or occasions when it is critical for you to give information or feedback to your manager, employees, or peers in your own or another department.

   _____

   _____

2. There are also occasions when it is important for employees to know how they are doing, how they can get better, what's going on, and why certain things are happening. List at least two specific situations or occasions when employees may want, need, or benefit from getting information or feedback from you.

_____

_____

3. What skills or techniques will you focus on when you are giving information or feedback to others?

_____

_____

7 | Delegation

*Proper delegation is an indication of a manager's trust
and faith in his people.*

—James F. Evered, *Shirt-Sleeves Management*
(AMACOM, 1989)

Delegation is the transfer of a task (and the authority to do it)
to an employee who reports to you. Since you are sharing your
authority (or power) with them, delegation is often described
as a way of *empowering* employees, broadening their responsibilities and your expectations of them.

Make no mistake! Delegation is *not* dumping your work on
someone else; it is *not* getting rid of tasks that you no longer
want to do by passing them on to someone else. If you need to
depend on others to help you get through your current workload, it is certainly within your rights to share tasks or assignments with your direct reports. This is not delegating, however.
Call it what you want, but it is not delegating.

Delegation is a strategic supervisory technique that can
provide a challenging new opportunity for an employee and a
time management opportunity for you. As William Marriott,
Sr., once said, "Good managers delegate. Don't do anything
someone else can do for you."

For many supervisors, delegation involves letting go of key
tasks and responsibilities that they do well, enjoy doing, and
formerly received recognition for doing. Therefore, technical
skill or operational expertise can actually interfere with effective delegation, especially if you try to hold on to what you
used to do while trying to fulfill your new supervisory responsibilities.

Delegation is really a question of using your authority strategically, a question of selecting the right opportunity to share your power with others. As mentioned in Chapter 1, the word *power* has some negative connotations, mostly because you can think of a number of situations in which the use of power was ineffective or the goals of power were objectionable. In its most neutral sense, however, power is "the capacity or ability to get things done, to exercise control over people, events, and yourself." You can use power in a negative way—by exerting power *over* others in an intimidating or threatening manner. Or you can use power in a positive way—by sharing your authority *with* others, by empowering them to do something on their own.

Power, therefore, is often based on perceptions: "What can you do to bring about results that will help you?" or "What can you do prevent results that will hurt you?" Your perceptions about power influence your decisions and determine how you will act in certain situations. Most effective supervisors have a healthy perception about power and understand the benefits of using their power in positive ways. They often define their leadership role as "the use of power to influence or affect others." They empower themselves by *sharing* their power, by empowering others. Their approach is best described as determining how much power they have in any situation and then deciding how they will use that power.

When you are determining whether you are comfortable delegating tasks to your employees (in other words, sharing your power with them), there are three key factors you need to consider:

1. *Think about your own experiences*—your own personal values and leadership inclinations. How much confidence do you have in your employees? Are you able to deal effectively with uncertain situations and still feel secure about yourself and the outcome of your team's work?

2. Then *think about your employees*. How ready are they to assume responsibility? Are they committed to organizational and departmental goals? Do they seem afraid of too much independence? Are they able to deal with risk and uncertainty? Are

they interested in new tasks or challenges? Do they have the competence—the knowledge and skills—to excel at this delegated task? Are they afraid of failure (or success)? Are you comfortable that you are seeing both high ability and a willingness to welcome new opportunities from a particular individual or from your group?

3. Next, *think about the situation itself.* How urgent, complex, and important is the task or assignment? Are you working under any extraordinary time pressures, budget constraints, or customer commitments? Does your organizational culture value and encourage delegation? What effect would delegating particular tasks have on both individual and team effectiveness?

There are several important benefits of effective delegation:

1. *Employees are given opportunities to develop new skills.* They are given ownership of new responsibilities and are challenged by the chance to make more important decisions. They may be motivated by your trust in them and your willingness to share your authority with them. They may learn a skill or develop a new competency that will help them qualify for a promotion or a more challenging project assignment in the future.

2. *You have the opportunity to develop employees,* to share your expertise, to help someone who reports to you become more self-confident and proficient. A direct result of delegation is that you have more time to concentrate on other challenging tasks delegated to you by your manager.

3. *Your organization has a deeper, more experienced pool of talent.* Individuals can function more effectively and more autonomously. Commitment, loyalty, creativity and teamwork are often byproducts of effective delegation.

Despite the many benefits and advantages of delegation, some new supervisors are reluctant to let go of tasks or activities they have done well for several or many years. They base their resistance on a familiar philosophy ("If you want a job done well, do it yourself") or on what may be perceived by others as an unfortunate self-fulfilling prophecy ("I can do it better myself!"). The question is not whether you *can* do the task or even whether you can do it better than anyone else. The real question for you now is whether you can afford to *keep* doing what you used to do. Remember that you have new responsibilities and challenges that will not allow you to continue doing your old job while doing your new one.

If you are not careful about this, your reluctance to delegate may put you in the untenable position of not being able to delegate. Your employees will pick up signs that you lack confidence in them, that you question their interest in doing the task that you used to do so well or their ability to do it. They will interpret your hesitation to delegate as a concern that they may fail or disappoint you. If they perceive that you are not willing to take the risk, they will probably conclude that the task is too difficult for them to accomplish.

Your employees, like most people, are probably already somewhat reluctant to have new tasks or assignments delegated to them. They may feel that they are overloaded or overworked, or they may lack the confidence they need to accept additional authority or responsibility. They may be afraid of failure or worried that new assignments could lead to criticism of their performance. They may have concluded that the incentives to do additional work are not worth the time and effort you will expect them to put in.

They may also have discovered that you are a helpful, supportive person—an enabler who wants your team to succeed—and that ultimately it is easier to delegate upward, to get your help with their work whenever they feel pressured or stuck. There are probably other reasons you can think of that your employees might be reluctant to accept your delegation. Deal with your personal obstacles first so that you can position delegation as a positive supervisory activity for both you and them. Focus as much as you can on some of the significant benefits:

- Sharing your knowledge, expertise, and authority is an investment that will pay off in the future for you, your employees, and your company.
- Someone else may actually have a better way of doing a particular task than the way you have always done it.

- You may actually enjoy the new aspects of your job—coaching, planning, monitoring the work of others—more than you enjoy what you used to do.
- You may get as much satisfaction from helping someone else succeed as that person gets from accomplishing something he or she may never have dreamed possible.

During my years of working with new supervisors, I have often used an analogy from my personal life to explain the benefits and challenges of delegation. I recall a time when my older son needed my help to tie his shoelace. He would appear, often at the most inconvenient time, and lift his foot in the air while asking for help. At the time, I was an expert "shoe tier," able to perform the task better than my son or his siblings. So I would whisk through the job, and in about two seconds, my son would have a neatly tied shoe that would stay that way until bedtime.

One day, however, when my son approached and raised his foot, I realized it was time for me to delegate this task to him. Although I could accomplish the task quickly (in less than two seconds) and effectively (a neat bow that would hold for hours), I knew it was time for me to help my son master this skill. He was ready, so I began helping him perform this task on his own. I knew immediately that this delegation effort would take time. First, there was some training involved. I demonstrated the proper way to tie a shoe, using examples ("The train goes through this loop and then backs up to form a bow") and encouragement ("Good try, you almost had it"). After a few minutes, my son stood up and proudly showed off his first solo venture: a glob of shoelace hanging precariously from the left side of his shoe. He pronounced, "There, I did it!" proudly, and I clapped at his initial success. "Let's see how long that one lasts," I said as he ran off to a new adventure. As I suspected, he was back in less than twenty minutes, eager to repeat the training process. We ultimately repeated it another fifteen times before he went to bed that night.

By the end of that week, however, he had mastered the task. His bows were still not as nice as mine, and it did take him slightly longer than it took me. But he was consistently getting the job done well, and he had even started adding a small flourish near the end of the task that was his own unique contribution. I can still see the smile on his face when he tied the shoe correctly for the first time. He beamed from ear to ear and simply said, "Yes! That's a good one." And I can still remember the feeling I had when I knew he had mastered this task and would not be lifting his foot to me on his wedding day years later. I felt a sense of accomplishment that almost equaled his.

Another thing I know in retrospect about this early delegation exercise is that it set the stage for future opportunities and interactions. My son and I had established a relationship based on trust and mutual respect that carried over into many of our later father-son activities. When it was time for me to let go of other things and not be overprotective, we were able to work together so that he got comfortable quickly and responsibly with new challenges—using sharp knives, lighting matches, driving a car, staying out late, being at home alone while his parents went away for the weekend.

If you want people to be and feel successful, you have got to start somewhere. No matter how insignificant the task may seem to you, it may be very important to them. Delegation requires the thoughtful matching of a task with the most qualified employee. Start by identifying technical tasks that you no longer need to do yourself, tasks that you may also not have the time to do anymore because of your new supervisory commitments. Even if you have only one person reporting to you, it is possible to delegate a challenging task that you believe this person is capable of performing.

In the following examples, notice how each supervisor focused on a particular task or activity, then matched it as precisely as possible with the right employee. Their delegation efforts, however, went beyond simply assigning a new responsibility to each of their employees. In each case, there were broader concerns and opportunities that the supervisors addressed.

Case Study

Brian is definitely Rosemary's best employee. She hired him herself about five years ago, and he has proved to be a competent and conscientious performer. He has excellent technical and interpersonal skills, and his consistently exceptional performance has certainly made Rosemary's job easier. She has more time now to concentrate on a few problems and to work with several new employees who recently joined her expanding claims department.

Whenever Rosemary needs to delegate an assignment or a new project, Brian is always willing, able, and available to help out. He usually gets the results she wants and comes to her only when he really needs help. Rosemary has rewarded Brian's performance each year with good pay increases, and he seems proud of the financial advances he has made in such a short period of time. He is definitely a "rising star," one of those exceptional employees who seem to have unlimited potential. In many ways, Brian reminds Rosemary of the way she was when she first joined the company.

Analysis

Before you read how Rosemary handled this situation, take a few minutes to jot down what you would do.

The Supervisor's Action

Rosemary has continued delegating new and challenging work assignments to Brian. She has been careful, however, to avoid two common pitfalls:

1. Occasionally supervisors can depend too much on their best performers, those employees who will come through no matter what. Rosemary wants to make sure that she is not taking advantage of Brian and that he knows how much she appreciates his hard work. She makes every effort to be sure that Brian does not see her delegating work as a punishment for his good performance.

2. Rosemary knows the danger of assuming incorrectly that Brian will be motivated by the same things that once motivated her. She wants to be careful of any casual comparison of the way Brian works with the way she worked earlier in her career. She intends to talk to Brian regularly to make certain she is meeting the unique needs of this excellent employee.

Case Study

Chris is a scientist who has worked for Steve in a research laboratory for approximately eight months. He is well educated and has proved to be extremely talented as a technical problem solver. So far, most of his assignments have put him in limited contact with other employees in Steve's work group. Since Chris seems to be somewhat of a loner, he has seemed satisfied working through problems on his own or with one or two of the more experienced scientists. Steve recently accepted a new research project, and he decided to delegate an important part of this assignment to Chris.

Analysis

Before you read how Steve handled this situation, take a few minutes to jot down what you would do.

_____

_____

_____

The Supervisor's Action

Steve's new project required Chris to work as a member of a larger team—probably seven or eight employees would play important roles in achieving the desired outcomes on time and within budget. Steve decided to delegate the report-writing component of this project to Chris. In addition to specifying how the reports needed to be structured, Steve took additional time with Chris to discuss the challenges of working with a team of individuals with different cultural and educational backgrounds, of different ages and genders, and with different amounts of work experience. He wanted Chris to be comfortable both with the assignment and with his new work team.

Case Study

Bill has worked for Owen for almost ten years. He has been a steady employee who sets a good example for all of his coworkers. Owen knows that Bill has been interested in advancement, but he really has not had a promotion opportunity to offer him. Recently, as a way of giving Bill some additional recognition for his past performance, Owen asked him to take a lead role on a special project team that will be making recommendations to senior management about a number of safety issues.

Analysis

Before you read how Owen handled this situation, take a few minutes to jot down what you would do.

The Supervisor's Action

One week before the safety team's first formal meeting, Owen decided to talk to Bill to see if he had any questions about chairing the meeting or identifying the most important issues for his team to focus on, or if there was anything else about this important assignment that he wanted to discuss. Although Owen focused on helping Bill prepare for his first team meeting, he made certain that Bill also felt comfortable talking about any concerns, challenges, or potential obstacles. Owen let Bill know that he wanted him to succeed and was willing to help. He did not, however, intrude on Bill's plans or indicate in any way that he wanted to attend or interfere with the meeting.

∼

The first step, therefore, in becoming effective at delegation is to identify the tasks or activities that one of your employees can accomplish. To determine which projects or assignments would be best for you to delegate, start by making a list of those tasks for which you are currently responsible. Get additional ideas by asking your manager or other peer supervisors for their suggestions about tasks they typically delegate. Remember that the biggest challenge may be your own willingness to let go of activities you enjoy doing and have received recognition for in the past. Be as honest as you can be with yourself about the items on your list, and classify them as:

1. A task you must keep because it requires your supervisory attention and because none of your employees is ready to do it
2. A task you can begin to teach one of your employees, but some additional development will be needed before you formally delegate the task
3. A task you can delegate

A chart like the one below can help you make your initial decision.

Task	Keep	Teach	Delegate
1.			
2.			
3.			
4.			

Delegation requires sharing your authority with your employees, empowering them to act as independently as possible.

Therefore, before you make your final decision about what to delegate and to whom, take a few minutes to make sure you are clear about how much authority you intend to delegate. How much autonomy and control do you want your direct report to have? There are several alternatives:

1. The employee has the authority to take action without your approval.
2. The employee has the authority to take action but must keep you informed of any decisions, problems, or unusual actions.
3. The employee must check with you about possible options before taking action.
4. The employee must check with you before taking any action.

If you are operating at the lower end of this list, take a close look at the task, the person you have chosen to do it, and your own concerns about letting go of this activity. Are you holding on to your authority unnecessarily? Are there unique aspects of this task that make it especially important to you and your work group, so that you are especially concerned about the consequences of failure? Have you picked the right person for the task? Once you have done this quick assessment, move on to a more detailed analysis of the task and the person involved in this decision. Be as thorough as you can in preparing for your delegation meeting. Effective supervisors describe this preparation stage as one of the most important components of successful delegation.

The next step is to describe the task or responsibility, then give some thought to the person you wish to delegate the task to. The following questions will help you do this effectively:

Description of the Task or Assignment

- What concrete, measurable results are required?

_____

_____

- How often or when must the task be accomplished? What are the current deadlines or time constraints?

  _____

  _____

- What resources (time, money, materials, equipment) are needed?

  _____

  _____

- What authority is needed? How will you transfer the appropriate authority for this task to this employee?

  _____

  _____

- What priority does this task or assignment have for the company or your department? Why?

  _____

  _____

- What procedures or methodology does the employee need to follow to accomplish this task?

  _____

  _____

- What additional information do you need to provide your employee to make sure he or she understands the task or the assignment?

  _____

  _____

- What are the benefits to you, the employee, or the company if this task is done well?

  _____

  _____

- What are the consequences to you, the employee, or the company if this task is not done well?

_____

_____

Once you have defined the task or assignment, spend time reviewing why you have picked this person for this task or this task for this person. Understanding why you see the match as beneficial will help you be able to explain your selection decision to your employee.

Employee's Qualifications

- What are the employee's current key tasks?

_____

_____

- What are the employee's best skills for this particular assignment?

_____

_____

- What relevant experience or preferences does the employee have when it comes to this particular task?

_____

_____

- What are the potential areas of difficulty the employee may need to address?

_____

_____

- What obstacles or barriers will you and the employee need to identify and address?

_____

_____

- What support or resources will the employee need from you or others in order to perform well?

  _____

  _____

- Will this task be a challenging and interesting development opportunity for this employee? How will the employee benefit from this assignment?

  _____

  _____

- How will accepting and accomplishing this task or assignment give this person satisfaction?

  _____

  _____

- What do you know from past experience about this person's ability to do new projects?

  _____

  _____

- How much detail will you need to provide this employee to ensure that he or she understands the assignment and gets off to a good start?

  _____

  _____

- What will motivate this employee to accomplish this task?

  _____

  _____

- What might cause this employee to be reluctant, resistant, or hesitant to accept this task or assignment?

  _____

  _____

Once you have prepared to delegate a new task or assignment to one of your direct reports, use the following action steps to orchestrate a successful meeting.

Step 1. State the purpose of the meeting. Discuss why this task or responsibility is important and why you have selected this person to do it. Start with a compliment about the individual's skills, talents, interests, or any other qualification that has made her or him a candidate for this new assignment.

Step 2. Describe the specific tasks, standards, and expectations associated with this responsibility. Describe the task in terms of key outputs, time frames, and the individual's need for autonomy or support. Remember to use language that is clear, concrete, and concise so that the employee knows what must be done, by when, and to what quality standards. Use examples or samples if helpful.

Step 3. Give appropriate authority. Share your power with the individual so that he or she feels empowered. Offer to formalize the transfer of authority if this will help the employee: "I will let the other department supervisors know that you have responsibility for this task starting next week so that they know they should contact you if they have any questions."

Step 4. Ask for questions. The employee may have concerns about his or her competence, acceptance by others, or current work priorities. The employee may feel a lack of confidence or have questions about your expectations. Encourage conversation, then be quiet and listen to the employee's concerns. Respond by working out ways to resolve or eliminate problems.

Step 5. Agree on a deadline, implementation schedule, and controls to measure progress. These should make the transfer of responsibility as efficient as possible for you and the employee.

Step 6. Ask for additional feedback and clarification. Before you close the meeting, give the employee another chance to talk about real or potential problems.

Step 7. Express your confidence in the individual's ability to perform the new task. Offer your help and support. End with a compliment that reinforces your decision to delegate this task to this person.

If the results of an assignment you have delegated do not meet your expectations or your own high standards, do not get discouraged. Most important, do not take back the task and do it yourself. Often, what is needed in situations like this is a careful review of what has happened so far with the delegated task. If you have not kept in touch with an employee about his or her progress toward achieving the desired outcome, now is the time to review the situation and determine where the breakdown occurred. Sometimes the employee's hidden concerns—fear of failure, lack of confidence, embarrassment about asking you for clarification—may have gotten in the way of his or her performance. Sometimes communication failures—unclear expectations, conflicting priorities, selective listening—may have gotten the employee off track, behind schedule, or over budget. Sometimes your own high standards—based on the way you used to do this task before you became a supervisor—may have created unrealistic expectations and a self-fulfilling prophecy about the employee's inability to succeed.

All of these problems can be identified and resolved satisfactorily without your taking back the task or assignment you have delegated. There is no reason to punish yourself or the employee because the initial effort did not work out as satisfactorily as you both hoped it would. There is also no reason to become "gun-shy" the next time an opportunity to delegate something to this employee comes along. Learn from your mistakes, encourage employees to learn from theirs, and do your best to get better the next time you delegate.

Over thirty years ago, Douglas McGregor published important research findings that characterized managers as either Theory X or Theory Y. According to McGregor's work, these two diametrically opposite types of managers have significantly different views about people:

1. *Theory X* managers believe that people are essentially lazy, that they dislike work and will avoid it if they can, and that they must be coerced, controlled, directed, and threatened with punishment to get them to perform. For this type of manager or supervisor, the average person prefers to be directed, wishes to avoid responsibility, has relatively little ambition, and wants security above everything else.

2. *Theory Y* managers, on the other hand, believe that people think work is as natural as play or rest in their lives and that they will give their time and energy to goals or objectives they believe in and are committed to. For this type of manager or supervisor, most people accept responsibility, want to use their imagination and creativity, and are willing to take reasonable risks.

If your personal inclination is to take a Theory Y approach to supervision, you probably also believe that most people engage in behaviors that they expect will lead to success and create a comfortable level of job satisfaction for them. You probably also agree, from your own personal experience, that individual motivation and personal morale are most often determined by some combination of the following factors associated with a person's job satisfaction:

- The amount of skill necessary to do the job well
- The variety and complexity of the work
- The degree of autonomy or empowerment involved
- The ability to control either methodology (how the work is done) or pace (how fast the work gets done)
- The degree of pride and commitment felt for the work
- The prestige of the job—visibility, status, and reputation earned
- The opportunity to reach new levels of achievement
- A realistic and achievable degree of challenge
- The amount of authority and responsibility
- The opportunity to make decisions and develop new talents

If you can match a potentially satisfying assignment with an employee who is ready, willing, and able to meet the challenge, you can have an immediate and significant impact on that individual's and your whole team's morale. Effective delegation can be the best way to create a motivating environment for all the employees who report to you. Try it out now. Before moving on to Chapter 8, take a few minutes to complete the following Journal Entry.

Journal Entry   **Date:** _____

Think about a time in your career when someone delegated an important assignment to you. Answer the following questions about this incident:

1. How did your supervisor's confidence in you make you feel?

_____

2. Did you successfully complete the task to everyone's satisfaction? What were the benefits to you and others?

_____

3. What effect did this one incident have on your future development, performance, and career?

_____

4. What did you learn about delegation from this experience?

_____

Take a few minutes to determine if there are other aspects of your job or additional areas of responsibility that you would like your manager to delegate to you.

_____

_____

_____

8 | Decision Making

No trumpets sound when the important decisions of our life are made. Destiny is made known silently.

—Agnes de Mille, American choreographer

Decision making is one of those ongoing activities that you now need to do in a very different way. As a supervisor, your decisions will face closer scrutiny—by your manager, your employees, and anyone who is affected by the choices you make. When you were an individual contributor, your decisions were probably less visible and less influential. Now other people will look closely not only at what you decide, but at how you make your decisions.

For Miller Curtain's controller, John Horan, decision analysis is an important skill:

> Part of my decision making process is first determining whether or not a decision is necessary. Sometimes the best thing is just to "sit tight" and do nothing. If a decision is necessary, I next ask myself if I have the authority to make the decision and, if so, do I have all the information required to make an informed decision. As a supervisor, you must use all of the information and input relevant to the decision, especially, if appropriate, the opinions of your direct reports. The key question sometimes is how much to involve others in the decision analysis process.

An analytical approach to decision making can help you keep things in perspective, especially when you are faced with important choices. Not that you will become quite as cavalier about the process as Harry Truman, who once said, "Not all decisions are going to be right. Whenever I make a bum deci-sion, I just go out and make another." However, the skills, tools, and techniques in this chapter can help you become adept at making good decisions. First of all, what makes a decision a *good* one?

The effectiveness of a decision is usually judged on the ba-sis of three criteria:

1. *Quality.* Is your decision the most effective way to achieve desired results? Is it a rational, logical approach based on available information? Of all possible options, is the one you selected the best?

2. *Acceptance.* Are people willing to execute your decision? Will you be able to rally support for your decision? Will those people who need to implement the decision be committed to its success?

3. *Efficiency.* How much time is needed to make and imple-ment the decision? Is this a decision you can and should make on your own without involving others in the process? If you need to meet with others, have you streamlined your process to ensure that you get the best, most acceptable decision as quickly as possible?

As a supervisor, you have choices about making decisions that will affect you and your work team. Depending on certain situational factors, different decisions may permit or even re-quire different approaches. For example:

• You may elect to rely on available information and make a decision without involving the individuals who will be imple-menting the decision. In this *directive approach*, you announce or tell employees what you have decided. Your role is deciding; their role is implementing.

• You may elect to review available information or collect additional data by discussing your pending decision with indi-viduals who can help you identify and weigh possible alterna-tives. In this *participative approach*, you are relying on others, either individually or collectively. Although you are still making the final decision, there is some involvement on the part of those who will implement your decision.

- You may elect to bring together everyone who will be affected by a pending decision and work toward a group conclusion. In this *collaborative approach*, the decision is acceptable in some degree to members of the group. Your role is to facilitate sharing of information, weighing and selecting the best alternative, and agreeing on a workable implementation plan.

- You may turn over responsibility for information gathering, analysis, and formal decision making to one individual or to a group. In this *delegating approach*, employees are given maximum involvement and ownership of the decision-making process, and your role becomes that of adviser or coach.

Effective decision makers, therefore, consider a wide range of options and vary their approach depending on the situation. The best decision makers:

- Are flexible rather than rigid, and choose from a range of decision-making options.
- Are aware of personal, group, and organizational factors in any situation. They realize that these factors are dynamic, and they choose an appropriate approach accordingly.
- Select an approach that best matches what their employees need and what they are able to give them.
- Realize that they need to balance a concern for production with a concern for people. They need to focus on both task and process issues and need to be concerned about both productivity and employee satisfaction.
- Keep in mind both the immediate issues and the long-range effectiveness of their group.
- Make certain that decisions are made—by the group when feasible or necessary, or by the supervisor if the situation requires.
- Let group members know how much say they will have in a given situation and how much weight their ideas will have on the final decision.

In many ways, that final point is the most important one for you to remember—the key component in any of your decision-making activities is letting your employees know how much influence they will have on a given decision. Clearly stating your role and your expectations of them will lead to more effective outcomes for everyone. Your decisions will be rational, acceptable, and efficient.

Listed below are several decision-making situations that supervisors I know have had to deal with during the first few months in their new jobs. Before reading how they made their decisions, take a few minutes to jot down how you would approach each situation, whether you would involve others in the decision-making process, and what you would say to let your employees know about your role and theirs.

Case Study

Kate C. supervises a group of eleven clerical employees in a large metropolitan hospital. In addition to record-keeping and billing activities, the group recently took on additional responsibilities for scheduling appointments for five doctors and preparing materials for many of the hospital's leading experts, who make frequent conference presentations. When her manager asked Kate to accept these new assignments, he estimated that they would take less than an additional eight hours per week, which she could share easily with her group. Kate was not sure her manager's estimate was realistic, but she felt confident that her team could handle these new challenges. The big question for her was how to distribute the work fairly so that all the work got done effectively and efficiently.

Analysis

Before reading how Kate handled this decision-making opportunity, take a few minutes to decide how you would approach the situation, how you would involve others in the decision-making process, and what you would say to your staff about their role in the process.

_____

_____

_____

The Supervisor's Approach

Because Kate realized that she needed information from her team about their current workloads and pressures, she decided to take a participative approach. At the beginning of one of her staff meetings, she told her employees about the new responsibilities her manager had asked them to accept. She told them that she knew this would be a challenging opportunity for all of them, that she had accepted the challenge on behalf of her team, and that she wanted to get ideas from them about how to handle these new tasks. She asked her employees to think about what they were currently doing and what would be the best way to incorporate these new assignments into their present work schedules. Kate presented several of her preliminary ideas and asked her staff to be prepared to discuss their ideas at their next staff meeting. She also told them that she would listen to their suggestions, incorporate them into her thinking, and develop a final plan that she believed would be a logical and acceptable way for all of them to meet these new expectations. Her staff would provide valuable information so that Kate could make a well-informed decision.

Case Study

Dan B. was recently promoted to supervise a small group of eight computer specialists he used to work with. When their previous supervisor left and the open position was announced, Dan was both the best qualified of the group and the only one interested in the promotion. The members of Dan's group are technically competent, but they have some serious interpersonal problems with their customers. Dan realizes now that he has probably known for a while that some of his former coworkers can be arrogant in their conversations with people who do not know as much as they do about computer applications. A few of these employees have a "take it or leave it" attitude about their solutions to their customers' problems. Three recent complaints about five different specialists have convinced Dan that he needs to do something quickly about this problem.

Analysis

Before reading how Dan handled this decision-making opportunity, take a few minutes to decide how you would approach the situation, how you would involve others in the decision-making process, and what you would say to your staff about their role in the process.

_____

_____

_____

The Supervisor's Approach

Dan decided to take a directive approach with his staff. He knew their current behavior was unacceptable, and he knew very clearly how he expected them to act in their conversations with their customers. Dan held a staff meeting. Without naming names or pointing fingers, he described specific behaviors mentioned by customers in their recent complaint calls. He expressed his concern that a know-it-all approach would affect their performance and damage their reputation. He talked about the impact their superior attitudes were already having on some of their best customers. He encouraged his staff to consider the implications of these negative behaviors, but he was very clear that they did not have an option about future customer service practices.

Dan was firm about specific behaviors and techniques he expected his staff to use in meetings with customers. He encouraged his employees to discuss any questions or concerns they had with him, either during their next staff meeting or in a private one-on-one meeting with him. This meeting set the stage and the tone for all of Dan's later supervisory interactions with his staff. He set the standards early, got a positive response from most of the employees, and quickly identified two individuals who lacked both the skills and the commitment to perform satisfactorily. In time, he found it easier to take a more participative approach because his staff had corrected their most critical performance problems.

Case Study

Christine L. supervises three assistants in a busy retail department store. They are extremely competent, confident, and conscientious in the way they perform their jobs. Recently, the store's corporate managers decided to change the current hours for all their mall stores. Christine knows that this change will have an impact on her staff. One employee is a single parent who needs as many hours as she can get with as much flexibility as possible. Another employee is caring for an elderly parent and has some constraints on available hours. The third and youngest employee occasionally asks for help from others because of his busy social schedule. All three will be affected by the new store hours—fewer hours during the week, more hours on the weekend.

Analysis

Before reading how Christine handled this decision-making opportunity, take a few minutes to decide how you would approach the situation, how you would involve others in the decision-making process, and what you would say to your staff about their role in the process.

_____

_____

_____

The Supervisor's Approach

Christine decided to take a delegating approach to this situation. She explained the new hours that would be announced the following month by company management. Then she turned over responsibility for creating a new work schedule to her competent employees. She offered to be a resource, a coach, if they needed her help. But she expressed her confidence that they could come up with a solution that would work for all of them. One week later, Christine's team had developed a trial schedule that all three of them agreed to and committed to with more enthusiasm than caution. Months later, with some minor adjustments, the schedule was working well.

~

If you decide to take a directive approach to making a particular decision, you may want to use the following action steps for individual decision making. If you decide to take a delegating approach and assign responsibility for a particular decision to one of your employees, you may want to encourage that person to follow these action steps as well.

Action Steps: Individual Decision Making

1. Define and state the decision that has to be made.
2. Review concrete symptoms or specific components of the issue, using known or observable data.
3. Gather the necessary information to analyze each symptom or component.
4. Determine which criteria you will use to generate and evaluate potential alternatives that can produce all desired outcomes.
5. Choose the alternative with the best cost-benefit ratio (the lowest negative–highest positive consequences).
6. Develop an action plan.
7. Announce and implement the action plan.
8. Monitor the action plan.

The Individual Decision-Making Process

Let's take a closer look at each step in the individual decision-making process.

Step 1. Define and state the decision that has to be made. This is the time to state what you want to happen in the future. What are you trying to accomplish? What must happen, by when, and why? Start by clearly defining what has to happen, then determine what you need to do to reach the end results you have stated.

Step 2. Review concrete symptoms or specific components of the issue, using known or observable data. What do you know about the situation, and what information gaps exist that need to be filled? Check your facts and make sure they are accurate, reliable, and appropriate to the situation. Be sure you are not basing your decision on hearsay, inferences, or assumptions. Be as objective as possible at this point so that your emotions and subjective biases do not interfere with the logical and analytical approach you are about to take.

Step 3. Gather information necessary to analyze each symptom or component. Determine the most efficient way to fill your information gaps. Talk to anyone who can help—peers, customers, your manager, your employees—but maintain objectivity and resist being unduly affected by a single opinion or perspective. Stay as open-minded as possible while gathering data. Also, put a limit on how much time you will spend on this activity and how much information you will attempt to collect. Beware of "analysis paralysis," the temptation to gather just one more piece of information, which can turn decision making into decision avoidance.

Step 4. Determine which criteria you will use to generate and evaluate potential alternatives that can produce all desired outcomes. List all of the criteria that will affect your decision. For example, is time a factor? Is cost important? How about the impact your decision will have on others? Once you have listed the criteria, be as specific as possible about how important each factor is and how you will weigh your options against these criteria. Some fairly common decision criteria include:

- Quantity
- Quality
- Cost
- Time
- Risk or safety
- Impact on others
- Compliance with regulations

Usually, you will have some document or factual data to help you define these decision criteria. Use a decision criteria matrix like the chart that follows to list both possible decision options and specific ways to measure their effectiveness.

Decision Criteria Matrix

Rating Scale: +/–/? or 1 to 5

Alternative Solution	Evaluation Criteria				Rating
	Time	Cost	Risk	Impact	

Step 5. Choose the alternative with the best cost-benefit ratio (the lowest negative/highest positive consequences). Evaluate your choice by using a standard cost-benefit analysis chart like the one shown on the next page. After you have stated the action you are considering, list all the benefits or positives that you can think of in Box A. Then list all the costs or negatives that you can think of in Box B. This will give you a quick snapshot of what might happen if you take this action. Then, repeat the process by evaluating what could happen if you do *not* take the action you are considering. List all the benefits of not taking this action that you can think of in Box C. Then list all the costs or negatives for not taking this action that you can think of in Box D.

Compare the boxes using the formula described below the chart. If the benefits of taking this action and the costs of not doing it (Box A + Box D) outweigh the costs of taking this action and the benefits of not doing it (Box B + Box C), you probably have a good action item. Do it, and do your best to manage the potential problems identified in Boxes B and D.

On the other hand, if the benefits of taking this action and the costs of not doing it (A + D) are outweighed by the costs of taking this action and the benefits of not doing it (B + C), you may not have the best action item. Do not take this action until you have taken a serious look at the items listed in Boxes B and D. If you cannot eliminate or reduce these negatives, you probably will want to skip this alternative.

Cost-Benefit Analysis

Action Being Considered: _____

	Benefits/Positives (+'s)	Costs/Negatives (−'s)
If I take this action	A.	B.
If I don't take this action	C.	D.

A + D > B + C ... Do it!
A + D < B + C ... Don't do it!
A + D = B + C ... Get more information

If you compare A + D with B + C and they seem to cancel each other out, you will probably have a difficult time convincing someone that this is a good decision. You may seem to be suggesting that the decision maker toss a coin to make a yes or no decision; however, what you probably need to do is get more information.

Step 6. Develop an action plan. Start by doing some careful contingency planning. Ask yourself, "What can possibly go wrong with my plan?" and list some of the factors that concern you at this time. For example, you may want to review some of the negatives or costs you listed in Boxes B and D of your cost-benefit analysis. Or you may want to consider recent events in your department or work area. For example, you will want to list any factor you have been having difficulty with in the past few months, such as equipment problems, employee absenteeism, late delivery of supplies, conflicting priorities, new customer demands, scheduling crises, and anything else that might interfere with your plan. Use a risk analysis chart like the one shown below to analyze the potential impact of each factor. List each contingency and describe a possible cause of this problem.

Risk Analysis Chart

Factor	Possible Cause	How Likely × How Serious = How Risky	Possible Effect

Use a mathematical formula to assign a point value to each factor and determine the risk involved. For example, try to define how likely the contingency is to occur, based on past experience. The following numerical ratings will help:

5 = This situation has happened often in the past and is very likely to happen again.
4 = This situation has happened occasionally in the past and is likely to happen again.
3 = This situation has happened infrequently in the past but could happen again.

2 = This situation has never happened but might.

1 = This situation has never happened and is not likely to happen.

Then try to assign numerical ratings based on how serious each factor would be. For example:

5 = Catastrophic: Would destroy the productive capacity of your work group.

4 = Critical: Your work group's productivity would be seriously affected.

3 = Detrimental: Your work group's productivity would be moderately affected.

2 = Aggravating: Your work group's productivity would be slightly affected.

1 = Nuisance: This situation would require minor attention.

Multiplying the appropriate numbers (how likely × how serious) will help you determine how great the risk of each contingency factor really is. For example, if the factor "has happened frequently in the past" (5 points) and would have a "critical" impact (4 points), the risk level (20) indicates that this is a contingency that you would need to address. If the factor "has happened frequently in the past" (5 points) and would be a "nuisance" (1 point), the risk level (5) would be less worrisome than that of other factors with higher scores. Once you have listed all the contingency factors you can think of, briefly describe the possible effects of each one. This should give you a complete picture of what can go wrong, why (causes), how risky each factor would be, and what impact (effects) these contingencies would have on your overall plan.

Once you have identified things that could go wrong and analyzed the risk, you can determine what actions you can take to either:

1. Prevent the problem from occurring (address the possible causes of the most important contingencies)
2. Minimize the impact if you cannot prevent the problem from occurring (address possible effects and create a "damage control" plan)

Incorporate your contingency plan into a complete action plan that includes the following considerations:

- Specific actions
- Clear responsibilities
- Realistic deadlines
- Clear target dates
- Coordinated sequence of activities
- Checkpoints for routine follow-up
- Reliable ways to measure progress and results
- Correctly defined priorities
- Feasible contingency plans

Goethe once said, "Thinking is easy, acting is difficult, and to put one's thoughts into action is the most difficult thing in the world." An action planning chart like the one shown can give you and others involved in implementing your decision a clear picture of who needs to do what, by when, and with what resources.

Action Planning Chart

Action	Responsible Person	Target Date	Resources Needed	Monitoring Technique

Step 7. Announce and implement the action plan. Make certain that everyone involved understands her or his role and its importance. It may be helpful to have a kickoff event to launch the official implementation of your well-conceived plan.

Step 8. Monitor the action plan according to the original decision outline. Keep an eye on the contingencies you identified, and be prepared to make any necessary adjustments. Hold people accountable for their part in implementing the decision by providing them with honest and accurate feedback on a regular basis. Provide recognition when it is deserved, encouragement when it would help, and constructive criticism when it is required to keep your action plan on track.

If you are concerned about the level of *acceptance* your decision will have, one of the three criteria mentioned at the beginning of this chapter, you may want to consider involving others in your decision process. People who need to implement a decision are usually much more committed to its success if they have played a role in formulating both the decision and an implementation plan. You will not need to worry about rallying support for your decision from people who have been actively involved in weighing key factors, discussing contingencies, and agreeing in advance on implementation responsibilities.

The action steps for group decision making are very similar to those used for individual decision making.

Action Steps: Group Decision Making

1. Discuss how you will make decisions during the process.
2. Establish a climate in which ideas can be shared.
3. State the problem, issue, or decision opportunity.
4. Gather necessary information from the group.
5. Analyze data and look for areas of agreement.
6. Consider the advantages and disadvantages of each option.
7. Select the best alternative by weighing both positive and negative consequences.

8. Devise a plan that identifies specific action steps, responsibilities, and time frames.
9. Implement and monitor the action plan.
10. Discuss the process the group used to make this decision so that you can repeat the positives and learn from your mistakes for the next time.

There are three significant differences between group and individual decision making:

1. You need to make a decision early in the process about how the group will decide things. Do you want unanimous agreement, or is consensus acceptable? Are there occasions when majority rule may be the best you and your team will be able to achieve? What is your role in the process, and how much weight does your opinion have on the final decision? Clarifying the decision process is an important first step in a group decision-making activity.

2. You need to establish a safe climate in which people feel comfortable sharing their ideas. If you are judgmental, critical, or controlling during the process, you may stifle creativity and raise questions about how involved you really want others to be in this decision. The negative effects are lower motivation, reduced enthusiasm, and resistance (rather than commitment) to the ultimate decision.

3. At the conclusion of this process, you may want to discuss how things went—what worked, what did not work, and what you can all learn from this activity to help you do better the next time. This is a good time to give your group recognition for their efforts and to hear their ideas about future group decision-making opportunities.

Whether you use an individual decision-making process or a group decision-making process, you will be held accountable more than ever before for the quality, acceptance, and efficiency of your decisions. Remember, there are other effective decision makers in your organization. Some of them—like your manager and some of your peers—might be good resources for you to refer to. Also, do not overlook your employees, some of whom make important decisions outside of work. For example, I recently met an individual at a manufacturing plant who was not included in an important decision about new computer equipment. He was told that this was a "high-ticket" decision that needed to be made by the "wizards" in Finance. He later told me that he would have been very comfortable being included in this selection process because, as treasurer for a national service association, he had just researched and purchased over a million dollars worth of computer equipment. In fact, he told me, he could have saved the company a lot of money because his research had found a less expensive alternative. He also said he makes decisions like this all the time. Try not to overlook some of the best resources you have who may be hesitant to volunteer but whose knowledge on a particular project may be invaluable. These individuals can make an incredible contribution and will feel valued when you ask. Their input can also make you look good. So be sure to ask.

Before moving on to Chapter 9, take a few minutes now to complete the following Journal Entry by evaluating one of your recent decisions.

Journal Entry   **Date:** _____

Write one of your recent decisions: _____
_____
_____

Take a few minutes to evaluate this decision by answering the following questions:

1. What level of *quality* did the decision have? Was it the most effective way to achieve the desired results? In retrospect, was the decision a logical, rational, and thoughtful response to the information available? _____

2. What level of *acceptance* did the decision have? Were people willing to implement your decision, or did you have to spend time rallying support for your idea? Did people resist the decision or show a lack of commitment to its success? _____

3. What level of *efficiency* did your decision have? Was the decision worth the amount of time and effort required to make and implement it? Did you streamline whatever process you used to get the best, most acceptable decision as quickly as possible? _____

4. On a scale of 1 to 10 (with "1" being a poor decision and "10" being an excellent decision), how would you rate this decision? ___

5. What would you do next time to improve your decision-making skills or approach?_____

9 | Problem Solving

In calm waters, every ship has a good captain.

—Swedish proverb

Along with communication and decision making, problem solving is the other supervisory activity that you will be required to perform on an ongoing basis. Once again, your approach will be much more public than it was when you were in a nonsupervisory position. You will be expected to make decisions about which problems to solve, and you will be held accountable for how, when, and why you arrive at particular solutions. Although not every decision involves a problem, every problem will require a decision. Therefore, effective problem solving involves a combination of the skills presented in Chapter 8 and the techniques presented for your use in this chapter.

First of all, you should be aware that you have choices to make early in any problem-solving process, choices that will reflect your initial reaction to a real or potential problem. In general, people respond to problems in one of three ways:

1. They use an *inactive approach*: Put on blinders, avoid or ignore the situation, and hope that it will simply go away with little or no personal attention, action, or involvement.
2. They use a *reactive approach*: Determine what has gone wrong, analyze the cause of the problem, and take steps to remedy the situation as quickly and as effectively as possible.
3. They use a *proactive approach*: Anticipate problems and develop contingency plans to prevent each problem

from happening or to minimize its impact if it should occur despite their best efforts to prevent it.

Obviously, the first approach is *problem avoidance*, not problem solving. Although there will be occasions when it will be best for you to wait before getting involved, you must make sure that your employees do not mistake inaction for avoidance or indifference. Turning your back on a problem will never solve it. Wishful thinking often leads to a worse conclusion: The problem gets bigger, affects other people, and requires a more complex solution in the end than it would have in the beginning. Consider the situation Jim G. faced when he became a new supervisor.

Case Study

Most of the people who reported to Jim were about his age, and he had comfortable working relationships with most of them. The exception was Ted, a veteran employee who was old enough to be Jim's father and occasionally acted that way. Ted often did what he pleased, and Jim's manager seemed to condone the behavior by saying, "You can't teach an old dog new tricks." There were several occasions when Jim needed Ted to follow specific procedures on a new project; however, he decided not to confront the situation and hoped for the best.

Analysis

Before you read about the consequences of Jim's approach, take a few minutes to jot down some of your thoughts about this situation and how you would handle it.

_____

_____

_____

_____

The Supervisor's Action

There were some initial problems, and Jim finally took a very hesitant and diplomatic approach. He started coaching Ted about what needed to be done, but Ted was resistant even when Jim knew he had offered useful suggestions. Ted continued doing things his way. Meanwhile, the important project was beginning to fall behind, and other members of the project team were becoming demoralized by Ted's obstinate behavior. Although no one came forward to say anything, Jim knew that everyone was waiting for him to do something about what had quickly become a much bigger problem. When Jim finally confronted the issue, he was angry and very assertive in his conversation with Ted. The bottom line, he emphasized, was that Ted had to follow strict procedures for the rest of the project. Jim's initial inactive approach thus created a stronger reaction than he probably needed to solve this problem satisfactorily.

~

The second approach to problem solving is much more common, and you may find yourself *reacting* to problem situations on a regular basis. This is an important expectation that comes with your job. Remember, however, that you are not expected to know all the answers or to have an easy solution for every problem. There are other people (your manager, co-workers, and employees) who can help. Your role is to bring the best people together to find workable alternatives when things are not going the way they should. Some problems will require your individual and undivided attention; some problems will require the expertise of others. Consider the situation Aleene M. experienced with Betty, one of the loan processors who reported to her.

Case Study

Betty had worked at the bank for more than twenty years in various administrative positions. She knew most of the jobs in the department and was very loyal to the company. She had developed good working relationships with most of her co-workers. However, she was sometimes selective about the people she got along with, and there were several employees who were hesitant to approach her for information or help.

Initially, Aleene talked to Betty about certain unacceptable work behaviors, especially making curt and sarcastic comments to employees from other departments. In the weeks after that conversation, Aleene saw noticeable improvement in Betty's interpersonal skills, and a number of her coworkers even commented about the change. She seemed much more friendly and approachable. Aleene also received positive feedback about Betty from employees in other work groups. There was, however, still one exception to the "good news" reports Aleene had been getting about Betty in the past few weeks. That exception was from Aleene's manager, who described his latest interaction with Betty as "blunt and discourteous."

Analysis

Before you read about Aleene's approach, take a few minutes to jot down some of your thoughts about this situation and how you would handle it.

_____

_____

_____

_____

The Supervisor's Action

Before discussing Betty's improvement with her, Aleene realized that she needed to get more information from her manager about Betty's "blunt and discourteous" behavior toward him. Aleene met with Lou and reviewed the incident in question. She discovered that Lou had stopped by Betty's workstation and asked her for a copy of last month's delinquency report. Because Betty was on the phone with a customer, Lou had jotted his request on a pad next to her computer and held it in front of her to read. Lou was in a hurry and needed the report right away. Betty turned her back on him and continued her telephone conversation.

After a few minutes, Betty ended her call, turned to Lou, and snapped, "Now what can I do for you?" Lou admitted that he had realized that Betty was busy and that he probably expected more attention from her than she was able to give him at that time. When Aleene asked if the customer on the phone had a serious problem, Lou said that it sounded "complicated" but not serious. Finally, Lou said that he had pretty much forgotten about the incident and would not have mentioned it except that he remembered that Aleene was keeping track of Betty's interpersonal behaviors and he thought Aleene would want to know about this incident.

Glad that she had found out some details about the interaction before talking to Betty, Aleene was prepared to give the employee encouraging feedback about her improved performance. She was also able to keep Lou's feedback in perspective by recognizing that her manager shared some of the responsibility for the relationship that he tended to criticize. Aleene knew that she would need to keep both Lou and Betty on their toes about ways to work together more successfully.

~

The third approach to problem solving is the best and the most difficult. Being *proactive* requires foresight and planning, both of which take time and energy. Many supervisors are so busy reacting to real or evolving problems (fire fighting) that they cannot afford the luxury of contingency thinking (fire prevention). Anticipating, averting, or minimizing potential problems can have significant payoffs for the supervisor who would rather head off a crisis than wait to meet it head-on. Consider how Marie W. anticipated what was going on with her best employee and took a proactive approach to a potential problem.

Case Study

Diane was definitely one of Marie's "star performers" in the marketing department of a large insurance company. When Marie hired Diane through the internal job posting system three years ago, she knew that Diane had potential, but Diane had already surpassed her expectations. She was conscientious and thorough in her work, she got along well with coworkers and internal customers, and she had made a favorable impression on senior management and on employees in other departments.

Although Diane had never mentioned the subject, Marie believed that she was ready for a promotion; however, there was really no place for her to go right now in the department. Marie was concerned that Diane might be worried about her career and look elsewhere for advancement. Marie hated the idea of losing her to another department or to another company. However, she knew it was her responsibility to recognize Diane's past performance and discuss her future career aspirations.

Analysis

Before you read how Marie anticipated this problem, take a few minutes to jot down some of your thoughts about this situation and how you would deal with it.

_____

_____

_____

_____

The Supervisor's Action

Marie acknowledged Diane's contribution to a recent project that was going to save the company thousands of dollars in the next few years. Marie pointed out how Diane's role had increased her visibility and credibility with senior management. Without mentioning promotion or any other type of recognition, Marie asked Diane how she felt about the recent project. When Diane talked about how much she had enjoyed the challenge and hoped that there would be additional opportunities like the one she had just worked on, Marie assured her that there would be other similar assignments for her in the future.

Diane responded, "I know that someday I will probably want to move up into supervision or take on some job with additional responsibility. But for now, I really love my work, especially the types of projects that others do not seem to want because they require interacting with senior management and some of our most demanding customers."

Marie said that she was happy to hear about Diane's interest in future projects, then told her that she wanted to recognize her past performance in three ways: by documenting her success in a memo to all the executives in their department; by recommending her for a special financial award for excellence in customer service; and by naming her team leader for a new project that the company president had asked Marie's group to handle. By anticipating a potential problem and raising questions about it, Marie was able to find out how Diane felt about her performance and the way she would be rewarded now and recognized in the future.

Problem Analysis: Understanding Causes, Effects, and Possible Solutions

Business more than any other occupation is a continual dealing with the future; it is a continual calculation, an instinctive exercise in foresight.

Henry R. Luce, publisher

When you are reacting to a problem that already exists, first ask yourself the following questions to help you determine the best approach to take:

- What will your role be in the problem-solving process? Will you make the final decision or contribute input to others who will? Do you need or want to involve your employees in the process?
- How urgent is the problem? How much time do you have to solve it? How much time do you have to work on a solution?

- How much money or other resources can you afford to spend on a solution? What are your budget constraints or financial restrictions?
- How will you evaluate the quality of possible solutions? What information do you need to help you establish criteria and give them an accurate weighting or significance?
- Do you want to involve others in the problem-solving process? Consider whether you want your manager, co-workers, employees, or customers to participate in the process, take accountability for the problem, and share ownership of the solution.

Once you have answered these questions and weighed all the factors affecting how you plan to proceed, use the following action steps to analyze the problem and develop a well-informed solution:

Step 1. State the problem as specifically as possible. Ask yourself questions like: What has gone wrong? How serious is it? When and where did the problem begin? Be as exact and precise as you can so that others have a clear understanding of the nature, scope, and significance of the problem.

Step 2. Determine the overall kind of information you need to define the real problem. Identify the most obvious and important symptoms, causes, and effects of the problem you are trying to solve. Select the best way to collect the information you need to proceed. Some popular data-collection methods include:

- Survey questionnaires
- One-on-one interviews
- Production or quality statistics
- Work sampling
- Technical experiments
- Time-and-motion studies
- Checksheets
- Observations
- Focus groups or staff meetings
- Brainstorming
- Benchmarking

Step 3. Collect the data you need. Discuss and document individual views, proven facts, and relevant symptoms until everyone involved agrees that there is a problem. Determine possible causes by looking for changes. Determine what factors are different now from the way things were before the problem occurred.

Step 4. Analyze the data for patterns or trends. Examine each possible cause independently and pick those that are most likely to be responsible for the current situation. Try to avoid value judgments or subjective criteria.

Step 5. Document your analysis in an understandable form and present it to those involved or to those in a position to help solve the problem. Discuss your conclusions and any implications of the problem that need to be dealt with.

Step 6. Identify ways to deal with the major causes of the problem or to minimize the effects the problem is creating.

Step 7. Develop a specific action plan with clear deadlines and responsibilities

Step 8. Test and monitor the action plan. If it seems effective, implement the plan. If it needs adjustment, revise the plan and then implement it.

There are many different problem-solving techniques available to help you analyze and solve actual problems. Here are several of the most popular approaches and a brief description of how and when to use each.

Brainstorming

Brainstorming is usually a group process. It works best when you want creativity, synergy, teamwork, and a comprehensive understanding of a complex problem.

1. The discussion leader clearly announces the focus of the session and states the problem that the group will be trying to solve.
2. A recorder writes down this key problem on a board or flipchart.

3. All participants throw out as many ideas as possible, usually in a rotational order with an option to pass if no new ideas come to mind.
4. All ideas are accepted without criticism and recorded without editing.
5. Participants build on the ideas of others. This triggers new thoughts, which can have a snowball effect.
6. The group taps the creative energy of each participant and produces synergy—the combined action of the group, which is more productive than the sum total of all the individual efforts.
7. Common elements are identified and discussed. Key ideas are clarified or combined when appropriate. Participants then vote on the most important ideas posted by the recorder.

Chronological Analysis

Chronological analysis is probably the most common technique for analyzing the history of a problem or examining trends related to a problem's development or intensification. Because there is often little room for discussion or debate about the data, this is usually best as an individual decision-making technique.

- What is the major symptom of the problem? _____

  _____

- When did it start? _____
- What happened then? _____

  _____

- What do you think caused the problem? _____

  _____

- Why do you think this? _____

  _____

- What happened next? _____
- Why? _____

• What needs to happen to get things back on track? _____

_____

_____

The Repetitive Why Worksheet

The repetitive why worksheet is an effective individual or group technique for probing more deeply into each known or suspected cause of a problem. It can be a useful technique for getting beyond the symptoms of a problem to the root cause of the situation.

• A fundamental symptom or cause of this problem is ____ _____

_____

• Which was caused by _____

_____

• Which was caused by _____

_____

• Which was caused by _____

_____

• Which was caused by _____

_____

• Therefore the root cause of this problem is _____

_____

_____

Force-Field Analysis

Force-field analysis is an effective individual or group problem-solving technique that is most useful when there are opposing forces or pros and cons related to a specific issue. This technique is used in situations that require changing direction, emphasis, or methodology. Once you have begun to determine causes and possible solutions, it can be a helpful tool for getting people to talk about their resistance to change or their reluctance to try new approaches.

Driving Forces		**Restraining Forces**
What do we want?	**vs.**	What don't we want?
_____		_____
_____		_____
What do we need? What are our goals, requirements, and motivators?	**vs.**	What obstacles exist? What are our areas of resistance and major concerns?
_____		_____
_____		_____
What forces lessen or minimize this problem?	**vs.**	What forces worsen or complicate matters?
_____		_____
_____		_____

The Proactive Approach

The final approach to problem solving—a *proactive* approach—involves anticipating problems and addressing them before they occur. Usually, you know from past experience that certain things can and will go wrong if you do not take steps to prevent these events from occurring. History will repeat itself if you do not take the appropriate action. The following action steps can help you analyze a potential problem and determine what to do now to prepare for future difficulties.

Step 1. Define the potential problem as specifically as possible. What are you concerned about and why? What are you trying to prevent or avoid? What are the potential consequences if the problem occurs?

Step 2. Identify steps that can be taken to produce a more positive outcome than the one you are anticipating.

Step 3. Weigh the benefits and the costs of significant contingent action. What are potential consequences of this action? What are the probability and the seriousness of these consequences (especially the negative ones)?

Step 4. Develop a workable action plan with clear deadlines and responsibilities. What must happen, by when? What might happen and why?

Step 5. Test and monitor your action plan.

John Gardner once said, "Most organizations develop a functional blindness to their own defects. They are not suffering because they cannot solve their problems but because they cannot see their problems." As a supervisor, you must have the vision and courage to see what is really going on in your work area so that you can confront or prevent problems. You must take personal responsibility for anticipating and adapting to change. You must be prepared to help make change happen effectively and efficiently. You will need to understand what is happening with your work and with the changes going on around you so that you can initiate changes that will improve quality, reduce costs, and save time. You will be held responsible by others for staying current about what's going on in your company and in your industry so that you can shift your approaches and priorities to meet the challenges you face.

The world is changing more rapidly than ever before, and adaptability has become one of your primary work priorities. Competition today often requires companies to shift from old and familiar approaches to something that is new and different in order to improve or survive. Change often brings problems and stress—things often get worse before they get better. But change can also bring positive results—new methods, better tools, greater opportunities, different challenges. Arnold H. Glasow, author of *Glasow's Gloombusters* and *Continuing Education in Aging and Health*, had this to say about being prepared for change: "The trouble with the future is that it usually arrives before we're ready for it."

If you want to take a proactive approach to problem solving, think about the different factors that usually affect your company and determine which ones can or will have the greatest impact on you and your work team. The following list highlights events or situations that many current supervisors believe may have a real or potential effect on their work groups:

- Global competition
- Technological advances
- New products or service options available to customers
- Company downsizing and reengineering efforts
- The shift in American business from a manufacturing to an information economy
- Government regulations that mandate additional company policies and procedures
- Aging facilities and equipment
- Increased budget constraints and limited resources (time, money, equipment, and people)
- Productivity and morale issues caused by interpersonal problems in a diverse workforce
- New company initiatives or priorities
- New equipment or systems
- Individual performance problems or conflicts about priorities, values, and work habits

In your new supervisory position, as you begin to anticipate potential problems and recommend alternative approaches, remember that many of the people who report to you will resist your efforts to bring about change. Many people are afraid of the unknown. They will resist anything new because they are afraid of failure. Some may be anxious about the possible loss of position, prestige, or control of the situation. Some may be frustrated by past efforts to anticipate problems and make changes. You may find them resentful, confused, or insecure about any new approaches. Others may express concerns about heavier workloads, conflicting priorities, their ability to meet your new expectations, or your company's stability, structure, goals, and strategies.

Successful supervisors often describe several techniques

that have helped them anticipate problems and implement changes. Some of these techniques may help you prevent a problem from occurring or minimize its negative effects:

1. *Stay focused on short-term goals and priorities.* Achieving small but early successes can build confidence in the change you are trying to implement and commitment to it. If appropriate, start by clarifying any new work roles and job responsibilities.

2. *Communicate messages clearly, accurately, honestly, and in a timely manner.* Don't be general or vague. Don't leave room for individual interpretation at a time when your employees may be relying on glorified memories of the past or predicting catastrophe for the future.

3. *Give employees frequent feedback about their progress.* Encourage calculated risk taking, and acknowledge any initiative taken by your employees that moves things in the right direction.

4. *Ask your employees how they feel about the change.* Recognize that there will be some resistance, and remember that it is better to discuss concerns and frustrations. If you do not lead or participate in these discussions, they will still happen, but you will not be able to influence what gets said. It's better to initiate these conversations than to try to deal with the loss of productivity that comes from low morale and persistent complaining.

5. *Listen more carefully than ever before.* Be accessible. Ask questions and demonstrate that you have paid attention. Deal proactively with rumors and incorrect information. Do not shoot messengers who bring you bad news. You need to hear the worst about what's going on before anyone else does—especially before your manager, other departments, or your customers.

Dealing proactively with change can be a big responsibility. Remember, however, that you are not in it alone. Depend on your manager, other peer supervisors, some of your employees, and other company resources to help you prevent potential problems and move your work group forward, implementing necessary changes. Keep things in perspective. Maintain a sense of humor and a sense of balance. Take things one step at a time, and be patient with yourself and with the employees you are depending on to make things happen. People around you will look to you for encouragement and support. Your positive attitude will make a difference. The comic poet Ogden Nash once said, "Progress might have been all right once, but it has gone on too long." When others feel frustrated and discouraged, they will look to you to set a good example and to keep a smile on your face.

Problems With People

Our main business is not to see what lies ahead dimly at a distance, but to do what lies ahead clearly at hand.

—Thomas Carlyle, essayist and historian

Like most organizations, your company requires a diverse group of people to come together to work toward common goals. Each person brings to the job a unique set of skills, values, attitudes, interests, and behaviors. Although you must work together with others, you are seldom able to choose the people you will associate with at work. Under such circumstances, problems can develop between individuals who must work together, but would prefer not to. Think about an occasion when you had a difficult time working with someone:

- What behaviors did you find objectionable?
- Why do you think the person acted that way?
- What was the impact of this person's behavior on you or others?
- How did you deal with this person?

Your answers to these questions may give you some insights into how to resolve problems that are directly related to someone else's behavior or performance. Actually, you can take one of two approaches: You can work with the person to correct the behavior, or you can develop a strategy to cope with the behavior.

The goal of these two approaches is the same: minimize the problem and maximize the use of your time, energy, and abilities. As in other problem-solving activities, start by analyzing the nature, scope, and significance of the problem. The following action steps can help:

Step 1. Define the problem. Describe the difficult behavior and determine how frequently it occurs. You may also want to determine whether the behavior occurs with others.

Step 2. Try to understand why the behavior is occurring and why it is annoying.

Step 3. Determine the impact that the behavior is having on you and others. List specific effects, such as lower morale, decreased productivity, or any other costs or negatives.

Step 4. Get agreement about a solution by discussing an approach that is appropriate to the situation with the person involved.

Once you have decided to confront and discuss the problem, the following action steps can help you resolve the issue:

Step 1. Schedule a meeting. Arrange for privacy and allow sufficient time to discuss the problem thoroughly.

Step 2. Describe the difficult behavior in a nonaccusatory way and state why it concerns you. Use specific facts and examples. Avoid offering your opinion about the possible causes of this problem. Focus on the behavior, not on the person or on personality.

Step 3. Listen carefully to check your understanding of the problem and its causes. Ask clarifying questions to make sure you understand. Ask probing questions to get a complete picture. Encourage the other person to respond by being patient and quiet.

Step 4. State the change in behavior that you would like to see. Be clear and specific about what you want or need. Be flexible if another alternative seems workable.

Step 5. Agree on an action plan that states specific actions and a timetable.

Step 6. Set a follow-up date and schedule time to review progress. If progress has been made, acknowledge the improvement and thank the other person. If the problem persists, revise the plan or consider new options.

When all else fails, develop a way to cope with the problem. Stay calm and try not to argue or accuse. Listen carefully and be sure you clearly understand what the other person is saying. Decide in advance what behavior you will and will not accept, and be firm about your position. Be persistent in your approach so that the other person knows that you are serious about the problem. Do not lose confidence in yourself or your ability to deal with people. Finally, look for ways to limit your exposure to this person so that you can reduce and control the negative impact the other person is having on you and your performance.

Approaching Problems as Opportunities for Continuous Improvement

Failure is the path of least persistence.

—Anonymous

No matter how carefully you plan your work and try to work your plan, problems are likely to occur. Problems are indicators that quality is missing from a process. Therefore, identifying problems, defining improvement opportunities, and conducting periodic problem-solving activities are routine steps toward improving quality in the way you and your group perform.

Some people act quickly to solve a problem, basing their decision on past experiences, "gut feelings," and "quick fixes." Others analyze and analyze again, never getting to the point of even trying a possible solution until analysis paralysis sets in. Still others ignore the problem, hoping it will go away, because they do not have a clue about how to determine what is going wrong and decide how to fix it. Some people define a problem as a gap between what you would like to have happening and what is actually happening. In the past, many supervisors believed that a problem was something to cover up, something to get rid of, something to hide from your manager, and something that was someone else's fault. Today, many companies encourage their managers to have a questioning attitude and to view a problem as an opportunity for improvement, a chance to make things better.

To make an improvement, you have to start by understanding possible causes of the problem you want or need to solve. Ask yourself, "Why did this problem happen?" Invite people who are familiar with the situation, involved in the process, or interested in implementing a solution to meet with you. Discuss the problem and decide on possible solutions.

Determine as many possible solutions as you can, and be as objective as you can be in evaluating each option. Your objectivity will help others agree more readily on a course of action, will help you explain your course of action to others, and will give credibility to your action plans. Objectivity in finding solutions begins with defining the goal or end result you are trying to achieve—for example, "Reduce by 60 percent the amount of time engineers spend on the phone answering questions from the plant." State a goal or end result that you feel is realistic for the problem you are working on, then develop a list of solutions that will move you toward that goal.

The next step is to identify guidelines or criteria that solutions must meet if they are to achieve the goal. For example, some common factors are cost, time, and quality. You may want to create a matrix to help you weigh and evaluate your potential solutions. This approach is similar to the one used in the previous chapter to evaluate a decision.

Finally, develop a comprehensive plan that involves others, encourages commitment to make the solution work, and translates the best solution into actions. Once your plan is operational, you will want to communicate your quality improvement efforts to others in your company. Start by keeping your boss informed, then ask him or her who else should know. Your problem-solving, continuous improvement effort might be useful or helpful to others.

Document your efforts and keep interested parties informed about your progress. State the initial problem in terms of negative impact and costs to your work group, the company, and people inside and outside your department. Then state your goal for the quality improvement effort or problem-solving activity. Briefly explain the methods and techniques you used to explore the main causes of the problem and what you did to identify possible solutions. Provide data or supporting evidence that the problem and your proposed solutions are not your subjective opinions. Then summarize what gains you expect or goals you have achieved in terms of positive impacts on your work group, your department, or your company.

Before moving on to Chapter 10, take a few minutes to think about your current problem-solving opportunities and preferences. Use the following Journal Entry to help you capture some of your ideas about your inactive, reactive, and proactive approaches to problems in your work area. You may also want to get input from your manager, your peers, your employees, and maybe even your customers about actual or potential problems.

Journal Entry

Date: _____

1. Think about a time when you decided not to take immediate action to solve a particular problem:

   What was the problem? _____

   _____

   Why did you decide not to act on it? _____

   _____

   Were there any negative implications? _____

   _____

2. Think about the most recent problem you solved reactively:

   What was the problem? _____

   What was your solution? _____

   _____

   Describe how you arrived at a solution:
   - Alone or with others? _____
   - Any special techniques? _____
   - Did you have to sell your solution to others? _____
   - Were there any negative implications? _____
   - Were there any immediate benefits? _____

3. Think proactively about an event or incident that might be a problem for your work group.

   What is the potential problem? _____

   _____

   What have you and your group done so far to address it? _____

   _____

   What will you need to do soon to be ready to deal with this problem?

   _____

   Whose support will you need? _____

   _____

10 | Coaching and Feedback

Management is nothing more than motivating people.

—Lee Iacocca, former chairman, Chrysler Corporation

As a supervisor, you cannot do your job by yourself—you need to know what is going on with all your employees in all the jobs that report to you. It is your responsibility to know what people are doing, how they are feeling about their jobs, why they are behaving in certain ways, what they expect from you, and how you can help them get better results.

In many organizations, the process of defining and managing priorities with and for employees is an annual cycle of activities that begins with goal setting early in the year and ends with a formal appraisal late in the year. Once you and your employees have discussed goals and priorities, it is your shared responsibility to make certain your employees stay on track, moving toward the successful achievement of required or desired outcomes.

To manage priorities effectively, you will need to monitor and observe your employees on a regular basis. You will need to provide positive and supportive coaching whenever it is appropriate. You will need to provide constructive and helpful criticism whenever it is necessary.

Your primary role will be supporting your employees' ef-

166

forts. You will need to be accessible, to review priorities and expectations regularly with each employee. When necessary, you will need to provide additional support, such as training or on-the-job coaching, and additional resources (time, money, and equipment).

Throughout the year, it will be important for you to know what motivates individual employees so that you can match appropriate rewards to their individual interests and needs. You will want to make sure that you are not rewarding poor performance by ignoring or accepting it. You will also want to make sure you that are not punishing good performance by giving your better performers too much work.

You are now in a position to oversee ("supervise") the performance of others and to give them honest feedback about *your* evaluation of *their* work. Many supervisors consider this the most difficult part of their job. However, if you look at feedback meetings as constructive and supportive coaching opportunities, these discussions can be extremely valuable for both you and your employees.

There are several overall principles that can help. Feedback should be:

- Specific (not general) and descriptive of job performance or work behaviors (not the person)
- Based on objective, quantitative performance criteria (not subjective, qualitative value judgments)
- Given on a timely basis whenever an individual needs to hear from you (not reserved for annual appraisal meetings, when it is too late for an employee to benefit from your feedback)
- Based on facts, observations, and other known performance standards or expectations (rather than on inferences, hearsay, or personal biases and values that have not been discussed clearly with the employee)

Notice in the following examples how the speaker follows the guidelines mentioned above:

Don't focus on the person.	Focus instead on behaviors or results.
"You were careless throughout this report!"	*"There are three mistakes in these figures that I want to go over with you."*

Don't focus on generalities.	Focus instead on specifics.
"Your presentation was well received."	*"Your report on the new computer system contained all the information necessary for the group to make an informed decision."*

Don't focus on qualitative judgments.	Focus instead on quantitative details.
"You did a good job on those test results."	*"The test results were 100 percent accurate and completed on time in every instance."*

Don't "dump" or "unload."	Focus instead on your willingness to help.
"I'm sick and tired of the delays in this study. I want the problem fixed now!"	*"Let's see if we can resolve the critical barriers to completing the study before you miss the deadline."*

Don't use inferences or assumptions.	Focus instead on your observations.
"You must not know how to complete these budget reports right, or maybe you don't know how important they are."	*"These budget reports are incomplete. We need to talk about it so that they can be fixed."*

Although communication is important at all times, it is most important when there are performance issues and problems. Without effective communication, you and your direct reports can get stuck in nonproductive or counterproductive activities that will keep you from achieving your goals. Time and energy can be wasted avoiding, denying, or minimizing significant issues that should be resolved. The most successful work groups depend on strong interpersonal communication skills to build cooperation, collaboration, teamwork, and trust.

Willingness to listen is one of the hallmarks of a trusting communication environment. Although there are many techniques for effective listening, the following list highlights some of the best:

1. *Try to understand both the content of the message and the other person's feelings about the message.* Most people have difficulty talking clearly about their feelings, so careful attention is necessary. Ask clarifying questions if you are unsure about the meaning of the message. Ask probing questions to learn more about the content or context of the message. To be effective, you need to encourage the other person to express his or her point of view. That means you often need to withhold your opinion until you are sure you have heard and understood the other person.

2. *Demonstrate your intention to pay attention to the speaker.* Listen patiently to what the other person is saying, even though you may believe it is wrong or irrelevant. Indicate simple acceptance (not necessarily agreement) by nodding or injecting an occasional "um-hm" or "I see."

3. *Make sure you really understand the complete message.* Repeat or rephrase, in your own words, what the employee has said. This is a good way to avoid jumping to conclusions or getting into an argument. Restating the message you have received is a way to clarify words, meanings, and feelings. As a listener, you are sometimes simply acting as a mirror (reflecting what the person has said), which will encourage the speaker to continue talking. Occasionally you may need to make summary responses such as, "You think you're in a dead-end job," or "You feel the project manager is playing favorites," but in doing so, keep your tone neutral and try not to lead the person to *your* conclusion. You can respond without either rejecting or accepting what has been said. Your initial intention is to make sure you understand the message. Paraphrasing or restating gives the other person a chance to clarify the message if you have misunderstood it.

4. *Allow time for the discussion to continue without interruption.* Don't make the conversation any more authoritative than it already is by virtue of your supervisory position.

5. *Ask open-ended questions.* Sometimes you need to ask open-ended questions to make sure you understand what the employee is saying and feeling. Use open-ended questions like, How do you feel about . . . ? What do you think of . . . ? In your opinion, how should we . . . ? Since these questions cannot be answered with a simple yes or no response, they let the other person know that you want to hear more about his or her opinions and feelings—even if they don't agree with yours. Accepting the person's right to have a point of view does not mean that you automatically agree. As a listener, you can very easily sabotage an employee's ability to share feelings and information with you if you do not demonstrate your willingness to at least hear what the individual has to say.

6. *Listen for what* isn't *said.* Evasions of pertinent points or agreements that come too quickly may be clues to something the person really wants to discuss. Focus on the content of the message; try not to think about your next statement until the person has finished talking.

7. *If the employee genuinely wants your viewpoint and asks for it, be honest in your reply.* But in the listening process, try to resist expressing your own views because your opinion may affect what the employee wants to say. Reserve your evaluation or assessment of the message until you are certain you understand it clearly. Don't make judgments until you have received all the information. Then respond in a way that shows that you have listened carefully.

When there are performance issues, use a problem-centered approach to give your employee a sense of control over the problem and to provide an open climate for communication. Instead of making the employee feel dominated or manipulated, try to concentrate on encouraging the individual to participate in solving the problem. Assigning blame or making subjective comments about the person usually causes defensive behavior and hampers a problem-solving approach. Using nonevaluative comments, which simply state that a problem exists, usually allows the two of you to jointly discuss possible solutions.

Employees have a right to know how you think they are doing on their jobs. They need and want to know when and how they are meeting your expectations so that they can continue those actions. But they also need and want to know when and why they are not meeting your expectations so that they can get better. Whether positive or negative, honest and accurate performance feedback is the basis for your working relationship with each employee.

To help you make these one-on-one conversations as effective as possible, the following suggestions break down this critical communication process into six distinct action steps, each with its own specific rationale, purpose, and desired outcome.

Action Steps for Feedback Meetings

1. *Prepare.* Take a few minutes to define your objective and to make sure you are using accurate facts and observed behaviors. Talk in specifies, not in generalities, abstractions, or inferences. Be certain that you are not making assumptions or jump-

ing to conclusions. Put yourself in the employee's place, and try to anticipate any questions, reactions, or concerns.

2. *Present.* State the purpose of the meeting. Be clear about your intentions, your objective, and your desired outcome. Give information using facts, observed behaviors, or other available data.

3. *Listen.* Create an environment in which the employee will feel comfortable sharing information with you. Deal with barriers that can interfere with your conversation. Be aware of your nonverbal message. Demonstrate your willingness to pay attention to what the employee has to say, and observe how the employee is reacting to your feedback. Concentrate on what the employee is saying so that you can restate it accurately.

Ask clarifying questions to make sure you understand what the employee is saying and why. Ask probing questions to determine the reason for the message and your own reaction to it. To do this effectively, use open-ended questions like:

- Why do you think that solution will work?
- If we were to try your recommendations, what problems do you anticipate?
- That sounds like an interesting idea. How did you arrive at that conclusion?
- Why do you feel so strongly about this situation?
- What are some of the advantages or disadvantages of that approach?

4. *Respond.* State your reaction to the employee's comments as honestly and as helpfully as possible. Clarify what is acceptable or not acceptable in your assessment of the message and the situation.

5. *Commit.* Develop an appropriate action plan based on your original objective and any new information received during the meeting. Define results and establish means to accomplish these results: What will be done and when? How will it be done? How will you and the employee know when the proper results have been achieved? Get agreement from the employee on the action plan you want to implement.

6. *Act.* Take steps to follow through on your commitments. Implement and monitor the agreed-upon action plan. Keep any promises you have made during the meeting, and hold the employee accountable for doing the same. Set a follow-up date to discuss the outcome of this meeting and to revise or reinforce the action plan.

Remember, if a conversation is important enough to take your employee's and your time, some clearly defined outcome should result from the meeting. Interactions should result in action plans that can be implemented and monitored.

Periodic review discussions provide the day-to-day links between goal setting at the beginning of the year and the performance review at the end of the year. Progress review discussions are focused, planned, and formal meetings. The key to effective review discussions is the ability to recognize and analyze *what* is being achieved (results) and *how* those results are being achieved (performance). As you review both results and performance, you will reach one of the following conclusions:

- Results and performance are both acceptable (or better).
- Results are acceptable (or better), but performance is not acceptable.
- Results are not acceptable, but performance is acceptable (or better).
- Results and performance are both not acceptable.

A progress review is conducted whenever necessary and should take into account:

- Specific results achieved in relation to priorities
- Goal achievement to date
- Needed revisions to goals or priorities to reflect changing conditions
- A progress assessment to assure that there are no surprises at the year-end review

The discussions balance the concern for results and performance. Reviewing results is relatively straightforward if the goal has been documented in measurable terms. The difficult area for most people is assessing objectively *how* the results are being achieved. When you consider the quality of someone's performance, you are usually evaluating factors like safety, teamwork, interpersonal effectiveness, customer service, and other variables that are critical to an employee's job success today. Ideally, you have already defined and discussed these qualities or competencies with each employee, and you have decided how to measure progress and success.

If the performance or results are not acceptable, then you must find out why and remedy the situation. The best answers to the following questions are usually found through a joint problem-solving approach involving you and your employee. These questions can be very helpful in analyzing performance.

1. Does the individual know what is expected?
2. Is the individual aware that he or she is not meeting the established expectations?
3. Are there obstacles that are preventing the expected results and performance?
4. Does the individual *know how* to accomplish the goal or priority, or is there a skill deficiency?
5. Does the individual *want to* achieve the goal or priority, or is there a motivation problem or a "will deficiency"?

Feedback is a way of communicating information to an employee about his or her past performance. It is a way of reinforcing positive performance and suggesting changes for improvement. Performance feedback works best when it focuses on quantitative descriptions rather than qualitative judgments, the employee's current short-term needs, and observations rather than inferences or assumptions.

When giving feedback, be descriptive. Relate, as objectively as possible, what you saw the employee do or say. Give specific and recent examples to help the employee understand your perception of the problem. Be sure your nonverbal language matches your verbal message.

Be clear and straightforward, but don't use labels. Avoid using ambiguous or subjective words like *unprofessional* or *bad attitude*. Instead, describe the behavior you have observed.

Avoid words like *always* and *never*. Be exact and don't exaggerate.

Take ownership of and responsibility for your message. Using expressions like, "My manager asked me to talk to you about this," or "Human Resources requires me to conduct this review meeting" conveys to the employee the message that you are not in charge of the situation. Talk to people when they are most likely to be receptive to your message. Ask questions to be sure you have been understood.

Remember that giving feedback is part of a two-way communication process in which you and your direct reports work together to achieve shared understanding. Therefore, giving feedback may also require active listening. To ensure mutual success, eliminate as many distractions as you can and come prepared to listen to the employee.

Respond nonjudgmentally to the total process: the content, intent, and nonverbal communication of the person who is receiving your feedback. Summarize the conversation or ask the employee to highlight key points, especially any action items or performance agreements. Maintain an atmosphere that encourages the sharing of information so that you and your direct reports will feel comfortable giving and getting feedback.

Because specific language is such an important component of giving constructive feedback, think about the exact words you would use in the following case studies, which you read about in Chapter 4. Jot down key phrases before you read the actual words the supervisor used to handle each situation.

Case Study

George had worked in the purchasing department of a large manufacturing company for almost twenty years. His greatest strength was his relationship with vendors. He had known and worked with most of them for years. Despite strong encouragement from Bill, however, George was having a difficult time telling one of these vendors, ABC Supplies, that its products and services were not meeting the company's current quality standards.

Analysis

Before you read about Bill's solution, take a few minutes to jot down some of your thoughts about this situation and what words you would use in an interaction with George.

_____

_____

_____

_____

The Supervisor's Action

Bill decided to use a coaching conversation that combined "review" coaching (giving George feedback about his past performance) and "preview" coaching (helping George get comfortable giving feedback to vendors). Bill hoped that his coaching of George would be a model for the way he wanted George to handle his conversation with ABC Supplies. After getting agreement that George would have this discussion, Bill used the following words to show his support:

> George, I'm glad you've agreed to talk with Mike Morro at ABC. I know you and Mike go way back, so I'm sure this conversation isn't going to be an easy one for you. Why don't you highlight for me a few of the key points you want to make during your conversation? Recently, you and I have talked about three issues: cost, size, and design specifications.

Later in the conversation, Bill reinforced the specific details George was planning to discuss. Here is what he said:

> I think Mike will appreciate your honesty, especially when you describe the discounts we are now being offered by some of his competitors. I know he thinks of you as an old friend, and I'm sure he wants to keep doing business with us. The tone of your whole conversation is, "How can we continue working together, using our newest standards?" Showing him our new specs for the X-13 Assembler should also help him understand our inter-

est in using different metals in this component of our product. I think size is another important consideration, as you mentioned, and bringing a sample with you is a great idea. Mike should be able to make the necessary adjustments once he knows what we are looking for.

Case Study

Elizabeth and Dave were relatively new employees who had been working together for about six months on a special project team in Suzanne's sales department. Both had similar academic backgrounds and excellent technical skills. When they worked independently, each person's individual performance met all of the company's established standards for quantity, quality, and cost. However, whenever they worked together, they competed with each other for Suzanne's time and attention.

Suzanne knew that Dave and Elizabeth often argued publicly with each other and that their feuding was not confined to their own work area. The project team leader and a few other team members had described this competitive behavior as counterproductive and demoralizing. Suzanne decided to discuss the consequences of "bad-mouthing" Dave with Elizabeth.

Analysis

Before you read the words Suzanne used in this conversation, take a few minutes to jot down what you would say to this employee.

_____

_____

_____

_____

The Supervisor's Action

These are the words Suzanne used to summarize her concerns about this ongoing problem. Notice that the feedback is specific and based on observed behaviors. Of course, Elizabeth was given ample opportunity to discuss her actions. This example, however, is intended to focus on the language used by the supervisor.

> Elizabeth, as you know, I stopped by after your project team meeting this morning, and I was surprised to hear you talking with your coworkers about Dave's latest report. I know we discussed this problem just last week, and I was under the impression that you had agreed to give any feedback about Dave directly to Dave. We also agreed that you would let me know about any problems you were having with Dave that you did not feel comfortable approaching him about. That way, I could get involved if you wanted or needed my help facilitating that type of conversation. So what happened today?

The conversation continued after Elizabeth accused Dave of similar behaviors:

> I'm concerned to hear you say that Dave spends time bad-mouthing you as well. But this conversation is really about your performance and not his, so let's stay focused on what you can do to improve this situation. The outcome of this project is very important. It's a great chance for you to shine. But you don't have to look good at Dave's expense. You need to figure out the best way to focus on your work and not worry about what Dave is doing. That's my job. So what can you do to correct this habit of criticizing Dave in front of other people?

Suzanne concluded the conversation by mentioning one possible consequence and encouraging Elizabeth to resolve the problem once and for all:

> This is the second time we've discussed this problem, and I need your commitment that it will be the last time. I would rather not reassign you to another project because I still believe this is the best one for you. But I need you working well with Dave so that everyone succeeds. If you are willing to commit to me that you will stop bad-mouthing Dave, we can give it another try for the next few weeks. What do you say?

Case Study

Recently, a number of factors had been affecting the quality of Andy's work group. Because of limited resources, a high volume of work, and some outdated equipment, Andy had been having difficulty motivating a good group of employees. In fact, one or two people had simply resigned themselves to the fact (and told Andy) that things would never get better.

Last month, however, one of Andy's veteran employees helped turn around this deteriorating situation. Andy was both surprised and pleased by her performance. Susan Malone had been in her position for a long time, and in the past few years she had become bored with some of the routine tasks. In fact, Andy had talked to her several times during the previous year about a decline in the quality of her performance and her somewhat arrogant and abrasive approach to customers.

In the past few weeks, however, Susan had assumed a leadership role with the team. She began setting a good example for everyone, including the handful of employees who seemed most cynical. Morale in Andy's work area changed dramatically. So did productivity, quality, and response time. Customers commented, and so did the department manager. Andy decided to compliment the whole team at his next staff meeting and to recognize Susan in particular for her outstanding contribution.

Analysis

Before you read how Andy handled this group feedback opportunity, take a few minutes to jot down what you would have said and done.

_____

_____

_____

_____

The Supervisor's Action

Andy began the meeting by reviewing the facts:

Last month's closing figures show a sharp increase in output and the lowest error rate we've had in over nineteen months. We've added two new customers, and at least three of our older customers have increased their purchases for next quarter by almost 28 percent. I know you've all been working hard, and I want you to know how much I personally appreciate your effort.

He continued by focusing his compliments on one individual:

I would like to give special attention to one member of our team for her excellent individual performance during the past few weeks. I warned Susan that I wanted to give her some public recognition today, and she told me that what she's done is "no big deal." Well, I disagree, and I just want to say "Thanks, Susan" for an outstanding effort on our behalf.

Andy concluded the meeting by letting his team know that the department manager knew about their improvement. He also discussed some potential benefits of the team's recent performance, and encouraged them to keep up the good work.

Jim is aware that our recent success did not come easily, that we are still struggling with limited resources and outdated equipment. The good news is that he has requested information from our vendors about new support systems and software. We're supposed to get an update about what's available early next month. Again, no promises, but I'm more optimistic than I was in December that we will be first in line for any new equipment.

~

In your own interactions with your employees, remember that specific language is a critical component of giving constructive feedback. Thoughtful preparation in which you determine the exact words you intend to use to start the conversation will help make the conversation more natural and more successful.

Root-Cause Analysis

When you are giving an employee constructive feedback about his or her performance, it is important for you and the employee to work together to determine the real causes of the problem. The best manager I ever had once told me that there are only six things that ever go wrong with a person's performance. These six factors can be a useful jumping-off point when you and an employee begin to examine the possible causes of actual performance problems. Root-cause analysis is a systematic approach to determining the basic underlying cause of a problem or incident so that it can be corrected and not repeated. This type of analysis can help both you and your employee isolate and examine the key factors in the situation. Consider the following six areas when you are trying to understand and resolve a performance problem:

1. *Trouble with standards or expectations.* Are they inadequate, unclear, inconsistent, or outdated? Have you communicated them effectively to the employee? Are goals and priorities unattainable or unrealistic?

2. *Lack of adequate feedback.* Has previous performance feedback been prompt, timely, and accurate? Has previous feedback been understandable, acceptable, and useful to the employee?

3. *Performance barriers.* Are there physical or environmental problems? Is the employee struggling with insufficient resources, time shortages, or priority conflicts?

4. *Knowledge or skill deficiencies.* Have there been changes in work systems, techniques, procedures, or job expectations? Does the employee lack training or adequate information?

5. *Continued disincentives or inappropriate incentives.* Are rewards and recognition insufficient to motivate the employee to do good work? Are frequent organizational changes creating uncertainty and lower morale? Is it more rewarding for the employee to continue poor work habits because the incentives for change are not sufficient? Is the employee getting positive consequences from improper performance? Do long-term positive consequences outweigh short-term negative consequences?

6. *Personnel problems.* Is there a "will deficiency," such as a lack of loyalty, dedication, or commitment? Does the employee have difficulty working with others? Are there other family or

personal problems? Is it possible that there are drug or alcohol abuse problems?

Once you have discovered the root cause of unacceptable work habits, consider the best way to change the individual's negative behavior. There are four options:

1. Create more positive consequences for the desired behavior.
2. Remove the negative consequences for the desired behavior.
3. Remove the positive consequences for the undesired behavior.
4. Increase the negative consequences for the undesired behavior.

These options are listed in descending order of effectiveness. In other words, you will achieve greater results by increasing the positive consequences for the desired behavior, if this is possible in the particular situation. The least effective option, but occasionally the one that employees require, is increasing the negative consequences for the undesired behavior. Formal corrective action and other types of progressive discipline are examples of this last option, which could also include such things as demotion, transfer from a project team, or a zero annual salary increase.

Performance Coaching

You have been promoted to this position because you have been identified as a person with a good work ethic. Be careful not to fall back to doing what you used to do. It is difficult to tell someone you used to work with what to do or that his or her performance is not up to par. But that is now one of your primary responsibilities.

—Walt Chandler, an associate professor at West Chester University

The purpose of performance coaching and feedback is to help employees maintain or improve their job performance so that they meet or exceed expectations and feel successful in both what they do and how they do it. Coaching is a two-way process of sharing information, ideas, and suggestions with your employees. Feedback must be specific, timely, performance-based, supportive, and balanced—it should include both positive and negative or constructive feedback. Its purpose is to foster continuous improvement, professional development, and personal achievement. Relationships are at the heart of coaching and effective feedback. Mutual trust and respect are critical to the success of the process.

Most coaching and feedback interactions have three main components:

1. In the *preparation stage*, give attention to data collection and planning activities. Get a sense of "where are we now?" and "where are we going?" prior to convening the meeting.

2. In the *conversation stage*, give attention to reaching agreement about current performance and formulating action plans for continuing or improving performance. Establish a meeting environment in which employees can be receptive to your suggestions about opportunities for improvement. Together, discuss current achievements and determine ways to maintain or change performance.

3. In the *follow-up stage*, give attention to implementing and monitoring specific action plans. Observe the performance of your employees and give them ongoing feedback about actions or behaviors that should be continued or changed. Also encourage and empower them to monitor their own performance.

Effective coaching and feedback interactions give you and your employees opportunities to identify, analyze, and correct any gaps in performance. Working together, you can help your employees determine where they are going, where they are now, and what they need to do to get better.

These problem-solving review meetings can help identify

and deal with problems early. When you notice what appears to be a performance problem, do not wait for the problem to go away, as performance problems rarely do. Neither should you wait to address the problem at the end of the review cycle. It is important that you to take prompt corrective action. Here are some guidelines for giving constructive feedback and conducting a problem-solving review meeting:

• Prior to the meeting, familiarize yourself with all of the policies, procedures, rules, and guidelines associated with the topic you are planning to discuss. Prepare for the meeting by gathering facts, data, examples, and any other pertinent information that will help you describe the problem and work toward a solution.

• Use a problem-solving approach that allows the employee to have sense of control over the problem and provides a climate for open communication. Encourage participation and ownership: Ask for ideas about possible causes of the problem, and invite suggestions for ways of solving it. Encourage a questioning attitude and ongoing self-assessment.

• Be prepared to discuss the effect the problem is having on the employee, on you, and on others, both in your immediate work area and in other departments. If the problem is having a negative impact on your customers, be prepared to provide explicit information gathered from conversations with the people to whom you provide products or services.

• Talk about performance in a nonthreatening, nonpunitive way. Blaming or name calling will only cause a defensive reaction and damage problem-solving efforts. If you simply state that a problem exists, you and the employee can work together to find a solution.

• Identify the causes of the discrepancy before attempting to find a solution. Verify that the apparent problem is the real problem by asking questions and listening carefully to the employee's answers.

• Be open-minded so that analysis and investigation are shared activities. Often employees who have problems also have solutions. Your role may be to help the employee find the best solution (not necessarily yours) and to encourage commitment to correcting the problem.

• Be sure you want to help the employee improve. The employee should know that you sincerely want to help and that the desired outcome of your meeting is a satisfactory resolution of the current problem. If the employee attacks or blames you, stay calm and do not get defensive. Keep a problem-solving focus.

• Show empathy and understanding so that you foster feelings of cooperation, mutual respect, and support. It should be clear that you are meeting because you want the employee to succeed.

• Try not to overuse these structured job performance discussions. Many times, on-site coaching at the employee's work area can solve minor problems. Reserve these more formal meetings for the bigger problems.

Before moving on to Chapter 11, take a few minutes now to complete the following Journal Entry so that you are comfortable giving performance-based feedback to one of your employees.

Journal Entry   **Date:** _____

Think about a situation in which you plan or need to give constructive feedback to one of your employees. If you cannot think of an upcoming situation, try to recall one from the recent past. If you still cannot think of an appropriate opportunity, use a hypothetical situation based on something that could go wrong in the future. Use the action steps for feedback meetings from this chapter to plan a conversation:

1. *Prepare.* Take a few minutes to define your objective and to make sure you are using accurate facts and observed behaviors. Be certain that you are not making assumptions or jumping to conclusions. Put yourself in the employee's place, and try to anticipate any questions, reactions, or concerns.

```
┌──────────────────────────────────────────────────┐
│                                                    │
│                                                    │
│                                                    │
│                                                    │
│                                                    │
│                                                    │
└──────────────────────────────────────────────────┘
```

2. *Present.* State the purpose of the meeting. Be clear about your intentions, your objective, and your desired outcome. Give information using facts, observed behaviors, or other available data.

```
┌──────────────────────────────────────────────────┐
│                                                    │
│                                                    │
│                                                    │
│                                                    │
│                                                    │
└──────────────────────────────────────────────────┘
```

3. *Listen.* Create an environment in which the employee will feel comfortable sharing information with you. Demonstrate your willingness to

pay attention to what the employee has to say, and concentrate on how the employee feels about your feedback. Ask probing or clarifying questions to make sure you understand what the employee is saying and why.

---

4. *Respond.* State your reaction to the employee's comments as honestly and as helpfully as possible.

---

5. *Commit.* Develop and agree on an action plan based on your original objective and any new information received during the meeting. Define results and establish means to accomplish these results: What will be done and when? How will it be done? How will you and the employee know when the proper results have been achieved?

---

6. *Act.* Implement and monitor the agreed-upon action plan. Keep any promises you have made during the meeting, and hold the employee accountable for doing the same. Set a follow-up date to discuss the outcome of this meeting and to revise or reinforce the action plan.

11 | Performance Appraisal and Development

In order that people may be happy in their work, these three things are needed: They must be fit for it. They must not do too much of it. And they must have a sense of success in it.

—John Ruskin, English essayist

While constructive feedback lets your employees know how they are doing day to day, a performance appraisal is a planned, focused, and formal assessment. Performance appraisal is a systematic evaluation of an employee's achievements in carrying out the requirements of his or her job and attaining individual, department, and company goals over a sustained period (generally one year). The performance appraisal meeting is also an opportunity for you and individual employees to discuss development areas and to agree on goals for the coming year. Finally, a written performance appraisal provides the documentation to support company personnel decisions like promotions, transfers, and demotions.

Most likely, you will conduct a formal performance appraisal with each employee once a year. Successful supervisors often say that the mark of a successful performance review meeting is no surprises for either the supervisor or the employee. To that end, you should schedule periodic reviews whenever necessary and use the end-of-the-year appraisal meeting as an opportunity to summarize all of your previous meetings.

The key to an effective performance appraisal is *objectivity*. As a supervisor, you are evaluating the performance of the job by what is achieved (results) and how the job has been done (work habits or behaviors, such as attention to safety, company policies, and operational procedures). *Results* must be measured against established priorities and goals that are understood by the employee. *Work habits* are measured against acceptable and defined standards, such as company or departmental guidelines and your stated expectations about teamwork, interpersonal effectiveness, and other recommended work behaviors.

You should be as *specific* as possible and use examples to confirm your observations. Vague general statements such as "good, reliable worker" or "needs to improve attitude" are not helpful to the employee because there is no specific result or behavior that they reinforce. This type of wording in a formal review also conveys the idea that the review was done hastily or without a great deal of thought. There are a few other common pitfalls you should try to avoid:

- Do *not* try to evaluate something that is inferred, assumed, or implied. Instead, compare actual results to expected results and form a valid conclusion about job performance. You can also compare observable actions or behaviors to stated performance standards and reach an informed decision about the quality of a person's work habits. Try to base your evaluation decisions on what the person has done and on what you have observed or heard the employee do and say.

- Do *not* omit the essential or exaggerate the trivial. Instead, keep specific events in perspective so that one good or bad episode does not take on disproportionate importance. Also, because of an employee's past performance, supervisors sometimes tend to make biased decisions about a current incident or situation. If the employee's work history is excellent, for example, you might be tempted to overlook or excuse even a fairly significant problem or mistake (sometimes called the "halo effect"). On the other hand, if the employee's past performance has been marginal or problematic, you might be tempted to overlook or minimize a positive contribution (sometimes called the "horned effect").

• Do *not* force performance evaluations to a comfortable middle ground for your convenience. Expect and acknowledge differences in the performance levels of your employees. Recognize positive achievements and correct negative behaviors. Avoid individual biases (friendships or prejudices) that can distort your evaluations. If your company has a performance-based merit increase system, any evaluation compression that brings all of your employees close to the same midpoint average can damage the effectiveness of monetary rewards. If everyone gets the same moderate raise, there may be little financial incentive to do excellent work. There may also be a subtle message to marginal employees that their work is being rewarded satisfactorily and there is no need to improve.

In Chapter 10, you had a chance to read how three supervisors gave timely and specific feedback to employees during the year. Notice how these supervisors later incorporated those earlier conversations into their end-of-the-year performance appraisals.

Case Study

George had been having difficulty giving his vendors constructive feedback about the quality of their products and service. In April, after Bill, his supervisor, convinced him that he needed to be more honest with one of his "old friends," George corrected the situation. Bill complimented George then and was careful to include this improvement as an important part of George's final review.

Analysis

Before you read the words the supervisor used in this situation, take a few minutes to jot down the exact words you would use to begin this conversation.

_____

_____

_____

The Supervisor's Action

Here are some of the words Bill used in his formal appraisal meeting:

> George, as you know from previous years, this meeting is our opportunity to discuss your performance during the past twelve months. I know there are a number of things we'll want to review, but I'd like to start off with what I think is your major accomplishment: improved vendor relationships.
>
> I'm convinced that your new approach began when you met with Mike Morro at ABC Supplies back in April. I know that wasn't an easy conversation for you to have, but you handled it well and got Mike to understand and accept our new standards. Since then, ABC has improved its quality and its response time so that they meet our needs. You did a great job addressing that negative situation.
>
> As we agreed in our July meeting, I've been in touch several times this year with ABC Supplies and a few other vendors you deal with on a regular basis. I've already passed on to you most of their important comments. But let me summarize the feedback I've gotten from your customers in the past six months. Overall, vendors have described your work this year as effective, more assertive, and much more specific about what you expect from them. I think that speaks well for your new approach, and I want to encourage you to keep up the good work. I'll keep soliciting feedback from your customers on a regular but less frequent basis, and I promise to keep you informed of any important information I get from them.
>
> I have also seen noticeable improvement in some of your recent reports. They are much more specific and succinct. Let me reinforce what I mentioned to you last month: I would like to see you use your November status report as a model for all of your future writing. The information in that report was clear, concise, and logical. Your cover memo set the stage for what I was about to read, and let me know exactly what you intended to present in your report. Sometimes you still slip back into a writing style that is much more difficult to read and understand, but I know you're working hard to make your writing more effective. Some of these recent examples are proof that you can do a good job in this performance area.
>
> You've continued making progress with the computer, al-

though I think it may be time to focus on some of the more advanced applications. I know we've both been guilty of making that a low-priority item this year. Now that you've gotten some of these important vendor issues under control, maybe this is a good time to give more attention to learning and using our new software packages. I would describe your performance in this area as "adequate" for now, but there is certainly room for additional improvement. What do you think? It's something we might want to get help on from Mary or one of the other technicians. Let's put it on our list of open items for further discussion.

Case Study

Elizabeth had gotten into the habit of bad-mouthing Dave, one of her coworkers on an important project. Her supervisor, Suzanne, had given Elizabeth periodic feedback about this problem. Although the employee had made some effort, Suzanne still believed there was room for improvement and focused on this issue during Elizabeth's appraisal meeting. Notice how Suzanne kept Elizabeth's modest improvement in perspective, but continued to emphasize what behaviors she needed from employees and why.

Analysis

Before you read the words the supervisor used in this situation, take a few minutes to jot down the exact words you would use to begin this conversation.

The Supervisor's Action

Here are some of the words Suzanne used in her end-of-the-year discussion of Elizabeth's performance:

Elizabeth, as I mentioned to you the other day, the purpose of this meeting is to review your overall performance during this past year. Obviously, the key issue has been—and continues to be—your work on the Magellan project team. Since June, I have had regular conversations with Lee Jones, the project team leader, about your contributions to this important effort. I have reviewed all of his feedback with you. But I would be remiss if I did not summarize some of the key points with you here today.

In general, you have stopped bad-mouthing Dave. However, Lee is concerned that you still make occasional private, sidebar comments and that you often send nonverbal signals that you disagree completely with Dave's approaches. Lee is also concerned that your earlier feuding has set the tone for Dave's participation on the team. Lee believes that Dave has become hesitant to open up in front of you and other team members. From my own observation of Dave's performance, I share Lee's assessment, and I believe you are partly responsible for Dave's reticence. I think we need to address and resolve that issue with Dave.

During our periodic review meetings, you have continued to minimize this problem as a simple personality conflict between you and Dave. Although you have modified your behavior toward Dave, you have continued to point your finger at him as the cause of the problem. I think you still see yourself as the "victim" of an "unfortunate" misunderstanding.

My overall assessment is that you are still not taking this problem as seriously as you should and that you still do not accept that it has implications far beyond this project and this one coworker. I see your performance on Magellan and your relationship with Dave as pivotal factors in all of your future work assignments. I know that you've tried harder, and I have gotten feedback that there has been some improvement. I want to encourage you today to keep things going in the right direction with Dave. I also need you to take responsibility for ensuring that there are no future incidents that could negatively affect Magellan.

Finally, I hope you can recognize the importance of teamwork and cooperation in the way we work in this department. I know you are new and somewhat inexperienced with some of these interpersonal competencies, but we can't afford disruptive and nonproductive internal competition. We're all in this together. Technical expertise is only one of the factors that contribute to our success. Collaboration and mutual respect are also critical components of the way we want to do business. Let's discuss some of these issues, opportunities, and potential challenges. What can we do together to make it work? More specifically, what commitments are you willing to make?

Case Study

Susan Malone really came through this year for her supervisor (Andy) and her whole department. In her formal appraisal and their end-of-the-year conversation, Andy took special care to make sure that Susan understood how important her contribution really was. He also discussed the significant effects Susan's performance had on her coworkers, customers, and the company.

Analysis

Before you read the words the supervisor used in this situation, take a few minutes to jot down the exact words you would use to begin this conversation.

_____

_____

The Supervisor's Action

Here are some of the words Andy used to recognize Susan for her good work. Notice that he also used this conversation to introduce some new challenges and opportunities for Susan:

> Susan, I have been looking forward to your annual review more than any other meeting I've had in a long time. I can't thank you enough for the way you came through for the department this year. Your leadership and outstanding performance set the tone for all of us, and I have gotten some significant feedback about you from a number of different sources. Let me highlight some recent examples:
>
> - At least ten of your customers—and that's about 80 percent of your total customer base, isn't it?—have called to compliment the company on its new "response time" policy. I

know that most of that effort has been your own personal initiative, and I've let your customers know that it's more *your* performance than *our* policy. What a difference you've made in terms of reducing the number of complaints I've had to deal with this year.

- Just last week, a few of your coworkers came to me with compliments about you. These were independent conversations with Jane, Vic, and Lucy about occasions when they asked for your help and got both your time and some excellent suggestions. I like the fact that people in our department look to you for help and direction. In fact, I would like to formalize that somewhat if you are willing to discuss a modest job change for next year. I know we talked about a supervisory position a few years ago, and you declined at that time, for what you described as "personal reasons." Well, we don't have a supervisory job open right now, but I was wondering if you would be open to talking about a type of "project leader" position. It would have only a small effect on your paycheck, but it would have a big impact on the way we structure our work efforts for the next few years. It would give me a chance to reassign some of your more routine tasks and delegate some of the more difficult customer investigations directly to you. It would also give you more formal authority to do some training with a few of our newer employees. What do you think? Would you be interested?

I was talking with Jim yesterday before he left for the senior management planning meeting. He asked me to give you this congratulatory note and to include a copy of it in your file. He assured me that he will get together with you next week when he gets back to thank you in person for your individual contribution to the department's success last year. He also asked me to tell you that he intends to let the other managers know about your end-of-year performance, especially the turnaround you made with two of our most important customers. Jim said that, more than anything else, those saved relationships will give him the leverage he needs to bid on some new equipment for our department.

In all of these examples, the supervisors used language that was clear and specific. Much of what was covered in their end-of-the-year appraisals was based on earlier review meetings in which the supervisors had already given their employees some or most of this feedback. In my twenty-five years of work with new supervisors, one of the most common complaints I have heard about performance appraisals is that they take an inordinate amount of time and energy to do well. I have always recommended that supervisors take a close look at how they are preparing for these final reviews. If supervisors have not done periodic coaching during the year, these final meetings often require a great deal of imagination and memory—trying to recall and record exactly what individual employees have done throughout the year takes time and creativity. However, if supervisors have had regular feedback meetings with their employees and kept accurate records of these meetings, then the end-of-the-year appraisal is primarily a summary of the previous conversations. The final review meeting should be easier for everyone. And remember, one of the most important goals for these meetings is, no surprises! That is easy to accomplish if you and your employees have been talking with each other during the year.

Development Review

The toughest thing about being a success is that you have to keep on being a success.

—Irving Berlin, American composer

The final component of a year-end performance appraisal has to do with your new responsibility to train and develop your employees. There is an old Chinese proverb that says:

If you want one year of prosperity, grow grain.

If you want ten years of prosperity, grow trees.

If you want one hundred years of prosperity, grow people.

Employee development is an important supervisory responsibility and an integral part of your company's success. In many ways, the future of your company depends largely on how committed your employees are to continuous improvement in their current roles.

The overall objectives, therefore, of employee development activities are:

- To ensure the systematic long-term development of sufficient technical and leadership depth to fulfill your company's business mission and achieve key corporate objectives
- To coordinate human resource efforts with business planning, strategy, and operational performance
- To support effective staffing decisions by ensuring that the most qualified individuals are identified, developed, and selected to fill critical positions in the company

Of course, the responsibility for development does not (and cannot) rest solely with either you or your employees. Ideally, it is a shared process built on a relationship of trust and respect. It is a mutual responsibility based on ongoing communication between you and your employees about current performance and expectations, actual and required competencies, present needs and future aspirations, and the employee's current job in the context of his or her career interests and the company's long-term business needs. The term *development*, therefore, refers to a variety of structured learning opportunities, ranging from improving performance in the employee's current function to development aimed at future work assignments.

One premise of development planning is that supervisors are responsible for developing employees by:

- Creating and maintaining an environment in which personal growth can occur
- Giving encouragement, guidance, and support
- Providing coaching and feedback that reinforce positive behaviors and modify negative ones
- Identifying underdeveloped qualities or underutilized talents
- Fostering a sense of teamwork, providing information

about shared goals, and identifying individual opportunities for growth and improvement

The other premise of development planning is that employees are responsible for their own personal self-development. In this increasingly competitive world, employees are expected to improve their performance continuously and systematically. Development discussions emphasize the competencies (knowledge, skills, and behaviors) that employees need in order to improve their performance in the current job and to prepare for future changes.

In fact, personal job security is linked to continuous improvement. Employees who have an interest in another area of the company should share their ideas with their supervisors so that they can get the development guidance and support they need. Individual development planning should be an output of your ongoing coaching efforts. Development plans should be reviewed regularly to ensure that efforts are being made to maximize each individual's contribution to the company and to facilitate each employee's personal goals.

The purpose of an employee development discussion is to assess and plan for employee development. The desired outcomes are:

- Clarity about strengths and improvement areas
- Realistic development alternatives and activities
- Short-term developmental goals (focused on current job)
- Long-term developmental goals (focused on future interests)
- Specific action plans for implementation and evaluation

Because employees "own" their careers, you should act as a coach and a resource in these discussions. Employees are primarily responsible for their own development, but supervisors play an important supportive role by discussing the employee's personal and professional objectives, the company's needs, and the connection between desired and actual opportunities.

Development review discussions usually focus primarily on the employee's current position—new dimensions, challenges, or any expansion of responsibilities within the current job. There are several key questions you should ask yourself at this time:

- What technical components of the job need to be developed to ensure that the employee's knowledge, skill, and techniques are as current and effective as possible?
- What areas of interpersonal effectiveness does the employee need to modify or improve?
- What competencies does the employee need to develop to ensure continued success or to improve goal achievement in this job?
- Are the employee's growth and development plans consistent with your company's growth and development strategies or plan?

When it comes to development coaching, successful supervisors capitalize on their knowledge and experience. They listen to the employee's personal interests, give their honest assessment of the employee's potential to move into other specific job areas or assignments, reinforce current strengths that will help the employee in future opportunities, and encourage continuous improvement in areas where developmental efforts are needed. To be effective in development discussions, you should be willing to offer your employees the following support:

- Let them know what you think about their personal interests. Are they realistic? Why or why not?
- If an individual is interested in moving up in the organization, what do you think is the best next step, and when? What about after that?
- Are there some cross-functional jobs the employee should consider? What about your own job as a logical step in this person's career progression?

To prepare for a development review meeting with an employee, ask yourself, "What does this employee need to do to improve his or her current job performance and prepare for future job assignments?" Consult with your manager or your human resources department if you need additional assistance or information. The following process steps will help you clarify key points for this discussion:

1. Identify development needs based on your rating of this employee from your year-end performance appraisal.

2. Identify possible development activities that will help the employee achieve short-term results and work toward long-term potential. These activities may focus either on a specific technical competency or on an area of interpersonal effectiveness.

3. Review possible action plans to meet each identified development need. Options may include:

- Formal training programs
- On-the-job training
- A new task or responsibility
- Job rotation
- Attendance at company or professional association meetings
- Specific reading materials
- Anything else you can think of that will address the development need

4. Discuss needs, actions, and career interests with your employee as part of the process. Reach agreement about specific action plans, including a start date and realistic target completion dates.

5. During the coming year, be sure to provide time and support for the development activities you have agreed to with the employee during the year.

6. Review the employee's progress with his or her development plan regularly throughout the year, especially when a particular activity (training program, project assignment, or association meeting) has just been completed.

In the following case studies, notice how each supervisor uses the employee's current job performance as a basis for development planning.

Case Study

Lee has worked at a national pharmaceutical company for almost ten years. He is a steady employee who sets a good example for all of his coworkers. His supervisor, Joel, knows that Lee is interested in advancement, but he really doesn't have a promotion opportunity to offer him at this time. During Lee's latest annual performance review, Joel gave him positive feedback about his recent performance. At that time, they agreed to get together for a development planning meeting.

Analysis

Before you read some highlights from that meeting, take a few minutes to jot down how you would handle this conversation.

_____

_____

_____

The Supervisor's Actions

Joel: Hi, Lee. How's the Enterprise project coming along? Any more delays with Tamec Industries?

Lee: It's amazing. Ever since I talked to them about their delivery problems, things have gotten better.

Joel: Maybe they just needed to hear some objective feedback from you. I know they have always appreciated our business. I guess the feedback about their recent performance was easier to take when it came from someone they respect and trust.

Lee: I have been doing business with Tamec for over fifteen years. I'm glad they took my feedback—or rather, *our* feedback—seriously. It would have been difficult finding a replacement for them in such a competitive market. Thanks again for your help getting ready for that feedback meeting.

Joel: You did the hard part, and I'm glad it worked out well for everyone. It's always nice to find a win-win solution to a problem. In fact, that's what I'm hoping you and I can come up with in this meeting. We agreed to get together to discuss your personal development plan, and I think there are a few things we should make sure we cover. First of all, I want to suggest that we continue working on some action items that we started addressing last year. Then I want to hear your thoughts about your current job and your future interests. Then I thought we would try to pull together our best ideas into a specific development plan that we can both commit to implementing over the next twelve months. How's that sound?

Lee: OK. So does that mean you want me to continue with some of the computer training I started last year?

Joel: I'm not sure you need anything that formal this year, but what do you think?

Lee: As I mentioned before, I thought the training was excellent. I got a lot of practical suggestions, and I really benefited from the hands-on experience. But it was very time-consuming, and it took me away from some key projects at key times. I guess I would like to try to find something a little less formal, less structured. I know I still need some help, but not nearly as much as I did last year. Maybe I can get by with some on-the-job coaching from Mary or Tom?

Joel: Sounds like a good idea. Let's keep a focus on improving your computer skills, but why don't you look into making some other skill-coaching arrangement? I know you've become more comfortable with your computer, and I have seen you using it well recently to help you juggle all those new priorities and administrative reports. I'm pleased with your progress—and I know you are, too.

Lee: I never would have guessed it would happen, but it has. And it really did help me with the safety project. I kept track of meeting agendas, minutes, and follow-up commitments. I managed my schedule better than ever before. Overall, the computer was a great tool.

Joel: And you know from your performance review what a great job I think you did with the safety project. Any thoughts about taking on another special project this year?

Lee: I would like to, but I guess that's really your call. The safety project was a great opportunity for me.

Joel: What did you enjoy most about it?

Lee: I guess being in charge of a fairly challenging group of people. It gave me a chance to try out my leadership skills in a safe, controlled sort of way. I knew that if anything went wrong, you would be there to bail me out. But I had confidence in myself and felt I could keep things on track. For years, I've wondered if I had what it takes to be a functional supervisor. Last year's project gave me a chance to try things on a small scale. Now I actually think I could do a good job as a supervisor, with some more experience and training.

Joel: I agree, Lee. You know there are no supervisory openings in our department right now. But that doesn't mean we can't work out an action plan to help you get ready if an opening does occur here or in another department, if that's what you want for your next career move. I think you have the talent to be a really effective supervisor. Why don't we talk about some of the competencies that are required for that job. Then we might be able to see how you can work on some of those skill areas this year. I have at least one project in mind. What are some of the skills you think you might want to focus on?

Lee: Time management and meeting management would both be high on my list. I know I've gotten better in both these areas, but I'm nowhere near where I want to be in those two areas.

Joel: OK, let's make sure those items are on your development plan for this year. I'll ask Human Resources for some information about available training programs or other training resources that might help. Once I get some information, we can review what's available.

Lee: And let's not forget the computer coaching you mentioned earlier. You're going to check into that, right?

Right. And when would you like to discuss that other project you mentioned?

Joel: I need to get some additional information from Research and Purchasing before we make any final scheduling decisions. I know the project is going to happen; I'm just not sure when. But I think it might be good for you to be involved from the very beginning, even in helping to select project team members from the other departments. You never know when one of those other managers may have a supervisory position open. You know I would hate to lose you, but there may be more opportunities in, say, Research than in our area.

Lee: I always thought I might wind up in Research someday. I've had some good experiences with people there.

Joel: Why don't I make some informal inquiries, then, while I'm setting up this project to see if there are any supervisory positions on the horizon? Meanwhile, let's document some of our agreements from this meeting. Then we can set aside some time next month to talk about any new developments.

〜

In this case study, the employee and his supervisor had a successful development discussion based on trust and mutual respect. Lee felt that Joel was truly interested in helping him make informed personal and professional decisions. Joel had taken the time to listen and to support his employee's development needs.

Case Study

As you read in Chapter 9, Diane has definitely been one of Marie's star performers. She has been conscientious and thorough in her work, and she has made a favorable impression on senior management, on employees in other departments, and on customers. Marie recently had a development discussion with Diane.

Analysis

Before you read some highlights from that discussion, take a few minutes to jot down how you would handle this conversation.

_____

_____

_____

The Supervisor's Action

Marie: Hi, Diane. As I mentioned yesterday, I wanted to get together with you today to discuss your personal contribution to the recent Paragon project. As you know, we are estimating that this research and design project will save the company thousands of dollars in the next few years. Thanks again for your significant effort on behalf of our department.

Diane: Thanks for the positive feedback, Marie. I really enjoyed working on that project. It gave me a chance to broaden my contacts with other departments and to learn some new diagnostic techniques.

Marie: Well, it certainly turned out to be a crucial project. And your involvement has really increased your visibility and credibility with senior management.

Diane: How so?

Marie: Don't tell me you haven't noticed all of the visitors to my office? There must be a half dozen senior managers who are interested in knowing about your availability for special assignments this year.

Diane: That's great news! Anything in the works?

Marie: Not really, at this time. I guess you know that with all of our recent reengineering efforts, there aren't any promotions available right now. There really isn't any other place for you to go right now in our department. And I would really hate to lose you to another department or to another company.

Diane: Well, I haven't been thinking about leaving here. In fact, I haven't even been thinking about a promotion. I guess what I was hoping we could do is talk about another assignment like the Paragon project, one that would help me learn some other aspect of our business. I want to be ready for a promotion opportunity when it comes along. But for now, I know I have a lot to learn in my current job.

Marie: Great. Let's review some of the opportunities my manager has been developing in the past few weeks. Maybe some of these projects will be in line with your long-term aspirations.

~

Marie has set the stage for future development discussions based on a clearer understanding of Diane's interests. Remember that professional and personal development does not always mean promotion. In fact, in today's work world, it often means expanding responsibilities within the current job role or function. Marie needs to be prepared to talk to Diane if any opportunities for promotion become available. Meanwhile, she needs to continue to find the right projects for a talented employee who is self-motivated and eager to work on diverse and challenging projects.

Case Study

Mark has worked at a large computer software company for almost twelve years. During that time, he has worked in several departments and has reported to three different supervisors. Mark is a good performer with excellent potential. His work is thorough, and he is conscientious about maintaining effective relationships with customers and coworkers.

Nancy has been Mark's supervisor for the past few years.

She has given him regular feedback about his performance, and has been an effective coach in areas where Mark has needed direction or support. During his recent annual performance review, Nancy complimented Mark on his recent initiative with several customers. That conversation got Mark thinking about his performance and certain new job competencies, so he asked to have a meeting with Nancy about his own development needs.

Analysis

Before you read some highlights from that discussion, take a few minutes to jot down how you would handle this conversation.

_____

_____

_____

The Supervisor's Action

Nancy: Hi, Mark. Thanks for taking the initiative to arrange this meeting. Why don't I just let you tell me what you have in mind?

Mark: Well, I think it all began with a comment you made last month during my review. You said that I did an excellent job recently when I approached some of our customers to find out what they would be needing from us next year.

Nancy: Yes, and I was especially impressed by the way you let them know about some of our new products.

Mark: That's what got me thinking about my own development plan. I think I can do even better in the area of customer service if I actually take the time to go out and visit some of my customers—you know, face-to-face meetings to help me understand how they use our products. If I had a better picture of what they need, then I would be in a better position to offer recommendations to help satisfy their needs.

Nancy:	It sounds like a great idea, but do you have the time to do it?
Mark:	I would have to be selective about which customers I actually meet with—some of the information I can get by telephone, especially from some of our smaller customers. But I do have a short list of "preferred buyers," and I really think it would help me do a better job if I actually went out to their locations for brief visits. I could do one a week for a month or so and get to see all of my biggest customers.
Nancy:	Tell me more about how these visits would help you improve your performance. Obviously, you have given this a lot of thought.
Mark:	Well, sometimes I think I'm shooting in the dark when I try to suggest either a new product or a variation on the way our customers are using some of our current products. A firsthand look might help. Then I could customize my suggestions to meet their needs. I agree that I took some initiative this past year, and it really paid off. But I think, in retrospect, I made it more difficult than it had to be. A personal visit might give us an advantage over some of our out-of-town competitors.
Nancy:	I could see where that would help. What else would be different?
Mark:	Sometimes I don't know enough about a customer's business to even know what to ask. It would be useful to see how our products flow into—and eventually out of—the production facilities. Again, I guess I could ask a lot of questions on the phone, but an in-person visit would be much better.
Nancy:	OK, you're being very convincing. How long do you anticipate visiting these customer locations, and what can I do to help?
Mark:	I think about two hours for each visit. Maybe, at first, we could go on-site together. When you go for one of your sales or planning meetings, I could go off for a tour and a meeting with the production

Nancy: manager. That way, you could help me prepare for the meeting, and we could compare notes on the way back. That would also help me get more comfortable with some of my negotiating skills. I need to influence their thinking and their purchasing habits, so it will really help me to get to know some of their production people better.

Nancy: Mark, I agree that this sounds like a very effective development strategy for you. I'm glad you took the initiative with this issue. Our conversation has helped me think about a few other possibilities that we should also consider. Now that we both agree that this is a great idea, why don't we work together to develop a specific action plan? Can we get back together again, say tomorrow afternoon, to identify the top three or four customers you want to visit? Then we can develop a schedule, a strategy for the meetings, and a method for arranging your visits. How's that sound?

Mark: Can we meet on Friday instead? I could use another day or so to think about where we should begin and what I want to accomplish once I get to meet these customers. I'm thinking now that every meeting might be different. Each one might actually have a different objective and a different strategy.

Nancy: Good point! Let's block out an hour before lunch on Friday.

∾

In this case study, the supervisor encouraged the employee to talk about his own development. Together they agreed on the best approach, expanded on a few good ideas, and arrived at a preliminary action plan that will produce excellent results for everyone involved, including Mark's customers.

At the conclusion of your own development discussions with your employees, remember to summarize agreements and next steps. Then, be sure to document a formal development action plan so that you and your employee have a clear understanding about:

- What will be done?
- Where will it be done?
- How will it be done?
- When will it be done?
- What must you do? What must others do?
- How will you know when it has been done satisfactorily?
- How will the employee know when it has been done satisfactorily?

This final step in evaluating an employee's performance sets the stage for ongoing improvement and development focused primarily on the individual's current job. However, this is also an excellent opportunity to give the employee a chance to discuss his or her future aspirations and present level of job satisfaction. There might be another development opportunity—like delegating a new activity or assigning this person to a challenging project—that will enhance a good performer's enthusiasm, commitment, and job satisfaction. Finally, depending on your own level of confidence and the degree to which you trust the information you might receive, this can also be an excellent opportunity to ask your employees for feedback about your performance during the past year. The best manager I ever had always asked me to be prepared to answer these questions about her during my end-of-the-year appraisal:

- What did I do this year, if anything, to help you achieve your current level of success?
- What could I have done to help you do a better job?
- What two or three things should I continue doing this year?
- What is the number one thing you would like me to change or try to do better?

These questions brought balance to this important conversation, and I was usually comfortable both getting feedback from this manager about my performance and giving her feedback about hers.

   Before moving on to Chapter 12, take a few minutes now to practice these techniques, using one of your current employees as a focal point. Complete the following Journal Entry by planning an end-of-the-year appraisal and development discussion with one of your employees. For an additional challenge, pick an employee who is currently doing average or below-average work.

Journal Entry   **Date:** _____

Think about one of your employees and do a quick assessment of his or her current performance. Answer the following questions as objectively as you can:

1. To what degree has this individual achieved the major results required for this year?

   _____

2. To what degree has this individual demonstrated the type of work habits required for his or her job?

   _____

3. What are this individual's current areas of accomplishment?

   _____

4. What are my current areas of concern?

   _____

5. What areas for improvement or development have I identified for this individual?

   _____

6. What can I do now to help this person continue good performance?

   _____

7. What can I do now to help this person improve?

   _____

12 | Conducting Effective Meetings

Business meetings are important. One reason is that they demonstrate how many people the company can operate without.

—Anonymous

When asked to describe their biggest time wasters at work, many people put meetings at the top of the list. The reason is obvious: Many business meetings are poorly planned and conducted. Often, the participants are not sure what the meeting is about or why they have been asked to attend. The meeting leaders are not prepared and are easily distracted into digressions by attendees who have their own agendas. In terms of lost or wasted time, the results can be staggering—very few of the ideas recorded at meetings are remembered at all; many of the ideas that are remembered are remembered incorrectly; and most of the ideas requiring follow-up action never get implemented.

Successful meeting leaders say that most group meetings fail for a number of reasons:

- Lack of planning and preparation by both the leader and the participants.
- Conflicting objectives: The leader's agenda is different from what the participants want to discuss or accomplish.

214

- Bad timing: There are other conflicting or distracting priorities.
- There is no real need for a meeting in the first place: Some regular meetings, like weekly staff meetings, are habitual and unnecessary.
- Too much time and energy are spent on venting, complaining, or finger-pointing rather than actual problem solving.
- The format of the meeting is not appropriate to achieve the desired outcome or accomplish the meeting's objective.
- Participants arrive with negative feelings about meetings in general caused by too many other (unsuccessful) meetings; there is resistance, cynicism, or reluctance from the start.
- The wrong people are invited; the right people are hesitant to participate because they are intimidated or embarrassed to offer suggestions or ideas.
- Too many people are invited; there is inadequate time for everyone to participate effectively.
- Participants are unclear about their role in the meeting.

A business colleague recently conducted this informal study in her company weeks after an important meeting. She asked participants what they remembered from the meeting.

- Less than 10 percent of the ideas recorded at the meeting were remembered at all.
- About 42 percent of the ideas that *were* remembered were remembered incorrectly.
- Some ideas remembered in great detail were covered only briefly at the meeting.
- Many ideas remembered were not discussed at all during the meeting.

Although the results of this study may be surprising, such results are fairly common in many organizations.

If you have any doubt about the quality of most meetings,

think about a meeting you attended or conducted recently. Evaluate its effectiveness based on the following questions:

- Did you know the purpose of the meeting before you arrived? Was the purpose or objective stated at the beginning of the meeting? _____
- Did the meeting accomplish its objective and result in some relevant action? _____
- What could the meeting leader have done to make the meeting more effective and productive? _____

_____

- What could the participants have done to make the meeting more effective? _____

_____

In addition, people who are disenchanted with the number and quality of the meetings they attend often wonder if there is any other, more cost-effective or time-sensitive way to do what the meeting leader was trying to do. Sometimes supervisors and other meeting leaders fall into a routine of meetings that are more habitual than helpful, more a custom than an option. Therefore, before you schedule a group or team meeting, make sure it is necessary and useful. Ask yourself the following ten questions to ensure that a meeting is the best way to accomplish your objective and to ensure that you get the maximum benefit from your collective efforts:

1. Is this meeting really necessary to help me and my group move forward to achieve our current goals?
2. What is the purpose of this meeting?
3. What positive changes would I like to see as a result of this meeting?
4. Who should attend this meeting, and what role should they play?
5. Who should lead all or part of this meeting?
6. What procedures or ground rules should be followed?
7. When and where should the meeting be held to ensure

minimum interruptions or distractions and promote maximum interest or participation?

8. What information should participants have prior to the meeting, and what should I encourage them to bring with them to the meeting?

9. What materials do I need for the meeting, including handouts, audiovisuals, and other supporting information?

10. How will the meeting activities and outcomes be recorded and reported back to the participants for implementation and monitoring?

The following meeting planner can help you keep track of all the important components of any group meeting you are planning.

MEETING PLANNER

Purpose:

Objective:

Who Should Attend:

Roles/Procedures:

Logistics:

When? _____

Where? _____

Agenda: Created _____ Distributed _____

Record Meeting Events: Self _____ Other _____

Possible Problems:

With the time I have selected: _____

_____

With the place I have selected: _____

_____

With the meeting topics or agenda: _____

_____

With the people who will be attending and the roles I have asked them to play: _____

_____

_____

What kind of disruptive behaviors do I anticipate (e.g., lobbying, sarcasm, dominating conversation, inappropriate joking, etc.), and how can I prevent these behaviors or minimize the impact they will have on others? _____

_____

_____

Many experts agree that there are a number of bad reasons for having a meeting. Before you decide to bring your group or team together, make sure your timing and your approach are appropriate by looking for the following conditions, which usually indicate that having a meeting is a *bad* idea:

- You have to act fast on an issue that is urgent, critical, or potentially volatile.
- You do not have enough information to make a meeting interesting or productive.
- You do not want or need reactions from others.
- The problem is between you and some other individual (do not bring a group together to discuss or try to resolve an issue that you can take care of with another person).
- There is a high level of anger or other emotion.
- You have already made a decision (do not pretend you are searching for a solution if you already have one).

On the other hand, many experts agree that there are a number of good reasons for having a meeting. Look for the following conditions to ensure that a meeting is appropriate, a *good* idea:

- You must be certain that your message is consistent and clearly understood by the group.
- You want or need immediate two-way communication.
- You need more resources, opinions, or ideas to be pre-

sented, discussed, and selected during a short period of time.

- You need creative thinking and collaborative problem solving.
- Others must carry out decisions, and a participative approach will ensure acceptance and effective implementation of the group's best ideas.
- You want to build up your team and develop ownership, commitment, and accountability.

Whenever you bring your team together for a meeting, remember that you are collecting, in one location, a group of individuals who probably have concerns about a variety of issues. In one-on-one meetings, you can focus on a few specific problems that an individual may be having with you, with himself or herself, or with other members of your group. In a team meeting, you are bringing together several people who may have problems with you, with one another, or with bigger issues, such as the company and its current policies, procedures, or practices.

When teams gather, there are important undercurrents that you need to be aware of so that you can address them comfortably. These hidden concerns usually fall into three main areas:

1. *Individual fit.* It is natural for team members to wonder or worry about how they are perceived by other members of the team. Common questions include: Do I belong on this team? Will I feel like an outsider? Will I be able to contribute? Will I be encouraged to contribute? How much influence or authority will I have? Will I be able to get along with and work with the other members?

2. *Interpersonal relationships.* It is natural for team members to wonder or worry about how members of the team will work with one another to accomplish the team's goal. Common questions include: Will team meetings be formal and structured, or will they be friendly, casual, and relaxed? Will team members be able to be honest with one another, especially when there is a need to give constructive feedback about inappropri-

ate actions or behaviors? How will team members make decisions, solve problems, and resolve conflicts? Will team members work well together, or will they argue, disagree, and compete with one another? Will team members like one another?

3. *Organizational support.* It is natural for team members to wonder and worry about whether the team's activities are important to the rest of the company. Common questions include: What is our role in the company's overall strategic plan? How will our efforts contribute to the "greater good" that will benefit us, other departments, and our company's customers or main constituents? How will our efforts contribute to the bottom line or to other current corporate objectives or initiatives? Who else in the company endorses, supports, or champions our efforts? Who else in the company, outside our immediate work area, will be holding us accountable for delivering quality results, on time, and within budget constraints?

Once you have decided to bring your group or team together for a meeting, review the following components of effective meeting management. These recommendations correspond with the action steps for one-on-one interactions described in Chapter 10. The same logical approach—prepare, present, listen, respond, commit, and act—works for both individual and group meetings.

Prepare

Before the Meeting

1. Clarify the purpose and the desired outcomes of the meeting. State an overall objective in action-oriented, result-specific language.

2. Identify meeting participants. Determine who should attend and why. Determine how each participant will benefit most from attending the meeting. Define specific roles—lead, contribute, participate—that you want each participant to play.

3. Decide on the process that you will use to accomplish the meeting's purpose. For example:

- Brainstorming to identify a variety of creative options to meet your current challenge
- Analyzing prepared information for patterns, trends, potential problems, or opportunities
- Group decision making by majority rule, consensus, or ranking options according to predetermined criteria

4. Develop the agenda. Set starting and ending times for each item. Be sure you have allocated an appropriate amount of time for each topic. If you are planning to build toward a decision, be sure you are not rushing through the process at the end of your meeting.

5. Send the agenda to the participants as early as possible. Include any other supporting information that the participants need. Also, remind them to bring any other information they will need.

6. Arrange for an appropriate room and the necessary equipment. Take care of any other logistical matters, such as food and beverages.

Present

During the Meeting

1. Start the meeting on time. Set the right tone and create an appropriate atmosphere.

2. Welcome the participants. Check in with them to make sure everyone is prepared to get started.

3. Review the purpose and desired outcome of the meeting.

4. Review your agenda:

- Recheck priorities and time allocations.
- Clarify topics (what you want to address).
- Clarify methods (how you want to accomplish results).

5. Establish ground rules that you want to follow during the meeting. Ask for input from the participants concerning other guidelines they may want to suggest.

6. Clarify the roles of the participants—minutes taker, timekeeper, leader, members, guests.

Listen and Respond

During the Meeting

1. Cover one agenda item at a time.

2. Keep track of nonagenda issues that come up that should be discussed later. Write them on a flipchart or meeting room board to remind yourself of these open items.

3. Set a pace that balances the complexity of the agenda items with the comfort level of the group.

4. Summarize the discussion on each agenda item before moving to the next one. Clarify or restate conclusions to confirm consistent understanding.

5. Test for consensus on each item.

6. Recognize and capitalize on the participants' appropriate behaviors:

- Some participants prefer to be task-oriented and will contribute by initiating discussions, gathering or giving information, and clarifying or summarizing key ideas.
- Some participants prefer to be process-oriented and will contribute by encouraging other participants, facilitating group discussions, creating harmony, suggesting compromises, or inviting others to participate.

7. Recognize and address disruptive behaviors. Some meeting participants may want to dominate conversations, lobby for their favorite solutions, or play games with you or other participants. You may also need to deal with self-appointed experts or condescending cynics. Deal with problems as quickly as possible. Try to anticipate what could go wrong before you start the meeting so that you are prepared to deal with these common problems:

- Small subgroups break into private conversations.
- One person monopolizes the conversation or tries to take over the meeting.
- Some people won't say anything.
- People arrive late.
- People are not prepared or are distracted by other work or personal issues.
- Key people cannot or do not show up on time or at all.

Robert Frost once said, "Half the world is composed of people who have something to say and can't, and the other half who have nothing to say and keep on saying it." As a meeting leader, your challenge will be to keep everyone focused on your objective by encouraging quiet people to talk and talkative people to listen. Gentle reminders from you can make sure that all of the participants are willing to contribute just enough of their best ideas to everyone else in the meeting.

8. Keep track of outcomes, commitments, and assignments. Take notes on your agenda sheet or assign a meeting "secretary." During the meeting, be sure to record information about:

- The exact time the meeting started
- The flow of discussion, giving credit to anyone who had a significant part in suggesting alternatives or affecting an outcome
- All outcomes, decisions, and assignments

Also record any agenda items not covered and note the exact time the meeting ended. Verify important information collectively or individually before the group disbands.

Commit

During the Meeting

1. Briefly review what you and the group accomplished during the meeting.

2. Summarize any decisions that were made.

3. Agree on what needs to be done, by whom, by when, and according to what policies or procedures.

4. Get preliminary input for your next meeting, including any old business or new agenda items.

5. Have participants evaluate this meeting—what went well, and what could be improved?

6. Thank the participants for their contributions and participation.

Act

After the Meeting

1. Record the outcomes of the meeting:

- Time/date/place
- Persons attending
- List of tasks accomplished, activities completed, problems solved
- List of new issues or problems: status and disposition
- List of assignments: what, who, when

2. Write and distribute meeting minutes promptly.

3. Carry our your assignments and monitor how others are doing with theirs.

4. Conduct individual or subgroup follow-up meetings to check for clarity, commitment, and the status of any tasks assigned during the meeting.

5. Provide individual feedback—positive to anyone who helped the meeting succeed, and constructive to anyone who disrupted the meeting process or who needs coaching to correct inappropriate behaviors before your next meeting.

6. Use input from the meeting and input from your postmeeting follow-up activities to plan and structure your next meeting. Review the ten questions mentioned earlier, and start by determining whether another meeting is necessary.

7. Set aside time for postmeeting planning (review notes from or about this meeting) and premeeting planning (review the status of current projects and any other possible agenda items for your next meeting).

Effective Meeting Management

Great minds discuss ideas, average minds discuss events, small minds discuss people.

—Admiral Hyman G. Rickover

As a supervisor, you will also need to be an effective meeting leader on frequent occasions. In general, here are a few suggestions that may help you prepare for this important role:

1. Whenever possible, anticipate and prevent group problems by dealing with them before the meeting or by preparing a strategy that will help you manage them during the meeting. Sometimes, premeeting one-on-one conversations with certain employees who have been disruptive in previous meetings will give you the opportunity to isolate and resolve an individual problem before it becomes a group issue. Sometimes, ground rules or meeting guidelines like "balanced participation" can provide a structured technique that will help you discourage rambling participants and encourage those who are hesitant to contribute.

2. Resist jumping to conclusions about the nature, scope, or cause of a problem. Sometimes it is easy to assume that one person's problem is really a group problem or that a group problem has affected each group member the same way. The best thing to do in these situations is test—ask good open-ended questions, encourage everyone to contribute opinions, and listen carefully to what your team has to say. You may even want to ask members to vote—publicly or by secret ballot—so that you have an accurate idea about how important and how widespread a particular problem really is. After the meeting, you can confirm in one-on-one meetings any lingering concerns you have about how an individual employee is involved with or affected by a particular problem.

3. Avoid exaggerating or minimizing problems brought to your attention during a team meeting. Because you probably have established a fairly tight, time-sensitive agenda for any

meeting, shifting gears into a problem-solving mode will not be easy and will more likely than not complicate your efforts to reach a suitable solution. One effective technique that has worked for many meeting leaders in this situation is to take a neutral, nonemotional approach to the problem by stating, "That sounds like something we should talk more about, either at the end of this meeting or in a separate meeting. For now, let me make sure I can restate the problem accurately, then let's agree to table it until we can give it our undivided attention. We have other agenda items to cover now, but I am willing to come back to this issue at the end of our meeting so that we can at least decide what we want to do about it next."

There are several ways you can deal effectively with disruptive behavior. One way is to do nothing and let the other team members take care of the problem. Your role, in that case, is to make sure that the individual behavior does not occur again and to confirm that the members of the team have interacted well with one another, with no additional repercussions. Another way to deal with disruptive behavior is to confront it "off-line," before or after the meeting. Your actions in these cases might include:

- Coaching—encouraging the employee to be more careful about an unusual performance lapse
- Constructive feedback—gaining commitment from the employee about resolving a recurring problem
- Assertive direction—letting the employee know about the negative consequences you will initiate if the unacceptable behavior occurs again

Effective meeting managers know that there are several common problems that can undermine their efforts and prevent them from accomplishing team objectives. Although some of their recommended techniques may be more appropriate than others in particular situations, a few of their ideas may be helpful to you when you encounter the following problems:

1. If your group is floundering, talk about the nature and cause of the confusion. Some members may be reluctant to make a decision or to support conclusions being presented by others. The group may not have a clear idea about what steps to take next. There may be a lack of clarity about the issues or a lack of commitment to the recommended actions. As the meeting leader, you may want to refocus energy and attention by asking the group open-ended questions like:

- What concerns do you have about our plan?
- What do we need to do so that we can move to the next phase of our discussion or process?
- What have I missed that is slowing us down?
- What other information do we need to help us feel comfortable about our next steps?

2. If your group is too eager to reach a decision or solve a problem, you may want to slow down the process and review how the group has agreed to work on this particular issue. Sometimes, one or two impatient participants can goad others into hasty decisions or discourage thoughtful consideration of other options. It will be important for you, as the meeting leader, to encourage patience, persistence, and a careful analysis of important details.

3. If your group tends to stray from the business at hand, you will need to bring it back on track as quickly and as tactfully as you can. Beware of Parkinson's law: "Work expands to fill the time available for its completion. The thing to be done swells in importance and complexity in a direct ratio with the time to be spent." Digressions and tangents may be symptoms that your group is trying to avoid a difficult problem. Unfocused conversations may simply indicate people's natural tendency to let their minds wander to nonwork interests or more enjoyable topics. It will be important for you, as the meeting leader, to refocus attention on your agenda. Make statements like, "We've strayed from our topic. Let's get back to where we were a few minutes ago." Or, "Let's summarize what we've been

talking about, decide what we need to do next, and move on to our next agenda item." It will be up to you to recapture the group's attention and energy.

4. If members of your group are feuding or competing with one another, suggest that they deal with their disagreements off-line, after your meeting. If these individuals report to you, offer your help if they believe they cannot resolve their conflict without some help from an objective third party. The best way to prevent disruptive interpersonal disagreements during your meetings is to anticipate them and deal with them before the meeting. Base your preemptive approach on past experience—"In our meeting tomorrow, I want the group to discuss a topic that the two of you have argued about in the past." Then try to define an acceptable ground rule that will help these employees disagree or discuss their differences without disrupting the rest of the group. If the adversaries cannot agree about appropriate behavior, you may need to be firm about not involving them in the meeting or in the part of the meeting that might cause a volatile reaction.

5. Some individual employees have a history of dysfunctional behavior in meetings—they use sarcasm, cynicism, passive-aggressive manipulation, dominating conversations, competition with you for the leadership role, or inappropriate humor to shift the focus of your meeting from your agenda to their personal agenda or needs. If you can anticipate these actions, talk to the offending individuals before your meeting and state clearly what you expect from them. Enlist their cooperation, but, if you cannot get it, consider more direct measures—not inviting them to the meeting or assuring them that you will confront their disruptive behavior publicly, during the meeting, in front of other participants. Both of these consequences might be embarrassing enough to get cooperation from these employees. If these negative meeting behaviors occur without warning, try to use established ground rules as a way of addressing them: "Thanks for your ideas, Mary. Now, in the spirit of *balanced participation*, let's hear what others have to say." You may also want to focus the group's attention away from the disruptive person. You can use body language—move or turn away from

this person—or address your next question to someone else in the group. After the meeting, be sure to give face-to-face feedback to the person about his or her inappropriate actions.

Remember, the best way to deal with group problems is to anticipate them and resolve them before they occur. This proactive approach will help your meeting run more smoothly. If problems surprise you during a meeting, you may want to take a brief break and deal with the issue or disruptive people immediately and off-line so that you can refocus attention on important agenda items. Finally, you will want to keep notes about what you learn during every meeting about structuring your next meeting and dealing with difficult participants.

Meetings do not have to be a major time waster for you and your work group. Think about the statistical significance of not doing things right—eight people attending an ineffective one-hour meeting waste an entire day of productive time for their company. There are many things you can do to reduce inefficiencies and ensure that your meetings are a valuable use of everyone's time.

Before moving on to Chapter 13, take a few minutes now to evaluate your current meeting management techniques. Use the following Journal Entry to plan your next group meeting and anticipate any potential problems.

Journal Entry   **Date:** _____

Think about a group or team meeting you are planning to have in the next few weeks. Prepare for it by using the following meeting planner. When you get to the end of the planner, list a few proactive steps you may want to consider to deal with potentially disruptive behavior from certain participants.

MEETING PLANNER

Purpose:

Objective:

Who Should Attend:

Roles/Procedures:

Logistics:

When? _____

Where? _____

Agenda: Created _____ Distributed _____

Record Meeting Events: Self _____ Other _____

Possible Problems:

With the time I have selected: _____

_____

With the place I have selected: _____

_____

With the meeting topics or agenda: _____

_____

With the people who will be attending and the roles I have asked them to play: _____

_____

_____

What kind of disruptive behaviors do I anticipate (e.g., lobbying, sarcasm, dominating conversation, inappropriate joking, etc.), and how can I prevent these behaviors or minimize the impact they will have on others? _____

_____

_____

13 | Evaluating and Managing Your Own Performance

If a man advances confidently in the direction of his dreams to live the life he has imagined, he will meet with a success unexpected in common hours.

—Henry David Thoreau, American writer

Effective supervisors project self-confidence and enthusiasm. They face problems optimistically, and they deal energetically with their day-to-day routines. They get the best from their employees and share credit for any successes the team achieves. They learn from their mistakes and help others maintain perspective about their own individual development needs.

Regardless of how long you have been in your current supervisory position, you will always be able to find some room for improvement. You will probably be more comfortable with certain aspects of your job than with others, and, occasionally, you may feel that certain tasks do not seem to be getting any easier. From my conversations with supervisors over the years, this is really an individual matter. Some veteran supervisors still have difficulty involving their direct reports in decision-making activities, while others have their worst times during the end-of-the-year appraisals. Some supervisors still struggle when they have to give an employee negative feedback, while others find it more difficult when they have to give someone positive feedback ("Joe already knows he's doing a good job, and he gets embarrassed when I tell him," or "When I tell Mary she did excellent work, she looks at me suspiciously as if I am trying to set her up for some bad news").

The challenge for you as you move forward in your supervisory career is to learn as quickly as possible which duties or responsibilities are (or will be) the most difficult for you. Start by identifying your strengths, and begin keeping a file of your supervisory accomplishments—good evaluations, complimentary letters from your customers, positive memos from your manager or other departments, your own personal notes about problem situations that you handled effectively. Focusing on your positive attributes is a good way to start because it gives you something on the plus side of the scale that you can use to keep things in proper perspective. Your personal development plan should build on your strengths and your successes. Knowing what you do well will help you maintain confidence while you work on areas that need improvement. If you are not completely certain about your strong points, ask for positive feedback from your manager, peer supervisors, trustworthy direct reports, and other professional associates who will give you honest information about your performance. Once you have established a base of "good news" about your current level of competence, ask some or all of those same people for their objective assessment of your developmental needs. If you would prefer asking for specific feedback about specific competencies, you can modify the self-assessment chart later in this chapter to help you focus attention on areas you would like to discuss with others.

Evaluating Your Own Performance: A Self-Assessment Tool

It is not the mountain we conquer, but ourselves.

—Sir Edmund Hillary, mountaineer and explorer

At the beginning of this book, you were asked to think about your role as a supervisor and to identify some of the competencies that would help you be effective in your new position. Now it is time to evaluate how you have done so far. Listed below are some supervisory skills and behaviors that you have been reading about and practicing. Although this exercise is intended to be a self-assessment, you may also want to ask your manager for feedback about how you are doing and how you can continue to get better. You may also want to ask one or more of your employees to give you some honest, useful feedback. There is room on the list for you to record and compare scores. Use the following scale to assess your current level of accomplishment:

Evaluation Scale

5 = Excellent level of performance
4 = Very good level of performance
3 = Acceptable level of performance
2 = Some need for improvement
1 = Great need for improvement
0 = Too early to evaluate

Coaching:

Consider how well you communicate openly with employees and give direction, feedback, and encouragement.

Your Self-Assessment _____

Your Manager's or Employee's Rating _____

Communication:

Consider how well you facilitate the flow of information. Do you deliver your messages clearly? Are you an effective listener? How well do you solicit information and feedback from others?

Your Self-Assessment _____

Your Manager's or Employee's Rating _____

Credibility:

Consider how well you deliver on commitments and take responsibility for the results of your actions. Are you perceived as honest, responsive, sincere, reliable, and trustworthy?

Your Self-Assessment _____

Your Manager's or Employee's Rating _____

Decision Making:

Consider how well you determine the scope, importance, and urgency of your decisions and act on issues in a timely way, using good judgment based on good information.

Your Self-Assessment _____

Your Manager's or Employee's Rating _____

Delegation:

Consider how well you assign tasks to appropriate employees, encourage employees to take responsibility for their work, and share your authority with them.

Your Self-Assessment _____

Your Manager's or Employee's Rating _____

Efficiency:

Consider how well you identify all tasks necessary to perform your team's work, determine critical tasks and priorities, and give appropriate attention to all the details required to ensure that the work goes smoothly.

Your Self-Assessment _____

Your Manager's or Employee's Rating _____

Flexibility:

Consider how well you adapt to change, demonstrate tolerance for uncertain situations, and use different approaches depending on different situational factors.

Your Self-Assessment _____

Your Manager's or Employee's Rating _____

Initiative:

Consider how well you anticipate needs and take action without being asked. Do you confront problems in order to solve them and assume responsibility for getting things done? Do you and your team initiate discussions with internal and external customers and then take action to meet or exceed their expectations?

Your Self-Assessment _____

Your Manager's or Employee's Rating _____

Innovation:

Consider how well you develop creative ideas and approaches for performing tasks, making decisions, or solving problems. Do you look for better ways to get the job done?

Your Self-Assessment _____

Your Manager's or Employee's Rating _____

Interpersonal Effectiveness:

Consider how well you create positive working relationships, foster a sense of cooperation among team members, and manage disagreements effectively.

Your Self-Assessment _____

Your Manager's or Employee's Rating _____

Meeting Management:

Consider how well you use meetings as an effective way to communicate information and to collect ideas from your team about important problems or issues.

Your Self-Assessment _____

Your Manager's or Employee's Rating _____

Motivation:

Consider how well you create and maintain an environment in which high expectations and high standards are consistently met. How well do you generate commitment from others? How well do you create positive working relationships by encouraging others to collaborate in achieving common goals?

Your Self-Assessment _____

Your Manager's or Employee's Rating _____

Performance Management:

Consider how well you establish performance goals with employees, observe performance, provide timely feedback, and prepare honest and thorough performance-based evaluations.

Your Self-Assessment _____

Your Manager's or Employee's Rating _____

Planning and Organizing:
Consider how well you establish a course of action for yourself and others, set priorities, adjust plans to meet changing situations, and anticipate problems.

Your Self-Assessment _____
Your Manager's or Employee's Rating _____

Problem Solving:
Consider how well you identify relevant information, gather and use facts, identify problems and possible solutions, analyze risks, and develop thoughtful recommendations based on available information.

Your Self-Assessment _____
Your Manager's or Employee's Rating _____

Risk Acceptance:
Consider how well you understand the scope of your authority, take accountability for your job, accept responsibility for successes or failures, and take action when apparent benefits outweigh potential costs or risks.

Your Self-Assessment _____
Your Manager's or Employee's Rating _____

Service to Customers:
Consider how well you know and meet the needs of internal and external customers; act in the customer's best interest; show concern for the customer's pressures, problems, and priorities; and measure the quality of service and satisfaction from the customer's perspective.

Your Self-Assessment _____
Your Manager's or Employee's Rating _____

Setting Goals and Priorities:
Consider how well you prepare realistic goals that are compatible with company and departmental objectives, determine and assign priorities, and achieve goals on time and within budget.

Your Self-Assessment _____
Your Manager's or Employee's Rating _____

Team Building:
Consider how well you create cooperation and teamwork to improve individual and group effectiveness; clearly communicate goals, roles, and responsibilities; and work to remove barriers to team effectiveness.

Your Self-Assessment _____

Your Manager's or Employee's Rating _____

Time Management:
Consider how well you use time to prioritize and schedule tasks effectively, how often you complete work within established time frames, and how effectively you eliminate your own time wasters.

Your Self-Assessment _____

Your Manager's or Employee's Rating _____

Your success as a supervisor will depend on how much credibility you have with the employees who report to you. As part of your ongoing self-assessment, ask yourself some tough questions and decide if you need to take any developmental actions:

• *Can you be trusted? Are you honest in what you say and do?* If you want to be perceived as trustworthy and credible, there is no such thing as "occasional" honesty or "situational" dishonesty. The truth—or the lie—will always catch up with you. Once detected, the dishonest moment can plague you forever and cast a shadow on every word you say from then on.

• *Is what you are doing consistent with what you said you would do?* People should know where you stand on important issues because your actions support your words. People around you should be able to understand your values and priorities because you keep promises and follow through on your commitments.

• *Do you communicate clearly to people who need to know what you are thinking and why you are acting in a particular way?* The words you use should not send mixed messages. Others should not misinterpret your suggestions or ideas as promises or commitments. Clarify and verify your messages so that they are not confusing or misleading.

• *Are you dependable?* There is no room for a double standard here. If you value dependability, you must make certain that it is a trademark of all your working relationships. Establishing a reputation for reliability requires consistent and careful attention.

After you have completed this self-assessment and requested performance-based feedback from others, take the time to create a personal development plan like the one you prepared for one of your direct reports at the end of Chapter 11. Start by defining a few SMART (specific, measurable, achievable, relevant, and time-bound) improvement goals for yourself. Do one thing every day, even if it seems like a very small step, to move closer to achieving your goals. Start a file to help you keep track of your successes. Start another file to help you keep track of your developmental needs; include brief descriptions of mistakes you have made, what you have learned from them, and any specific action you have decided to take in order to improve. Confront problems. Celebrate successes. Keep moving forward with confidence. Learn whatever you can from other talented and effective leaders in your organization. Look to those managers and supervisors who started off where you are today, then invested the time and effort to develop these important competencies.

By now, you probably have had numerous real-world opportunities to try out some of the skills and techniques highlighted in this book. We hope that the suggestions and examples have helped you understand your new role and helped you move forward as a supervisor with confidence and enthusiasm. Our hope for you is that some day, the people who work with you will be able to say what someone once said about Charles Percy, former president of Bell & Howell: "From the very beginning, he showed a knack for being able to get the most out of other people."

Good luck!

Journal Entry   **Date:** _____

Review all of your journal entries from previous chapters. Reflect on any key learnings you want to remember and, in the space below, summarize the actions you plan to take. Then develop three personal commitments you are willing to make as a result of reading this book.

Chapter 1 The Challenge of Being a Supervisor
        Key Learnings _____
        Action Plan _____

Chapter 2 Understanding What's Expected of You
        Key Learnings _____
        Action Plan _____

Chapter 3 Learning Written and Unwritten Rules
        Key Learnings _____
        Action Plan _____

Chapter 4 Motivation: Getting Commitment From Others
        Key Learnings _____
        Action Plan _____

Chapter 5 Setting Goals and Priorities
        Key Learnings _____
        Action Plan _____

Chapter 6 Communication
        Key Learnings _____
        Action Plan _____

Chapter 7 Delegation
        Key Learnings _____
        Action Plan _____

Chapter 8 Decision Making

Key Learnings _____

Action Plan _____

Chapter 9 Problem Solving

Key Learnings _____

Action Plan _____

Chapter 10 Coaching and Feedback

Key Learnings _____

Action Plan _____

Chapter 11 Performance Appraisal and Development

Key Learnings _____

Action Plan _____

Chapter 12 Conducting Effective Meetings

Key Learnings _____

Action Plan _____

Commitments:

1. _____

_____

_____

2. _____

_____

_____

3. _____

_____

_____

Personal Development Priorities:

_____

_____

_____

_____

Index

alignment, 75
appraisal, *see* performance appraisal

Barth, Tony
  on effective supervising, 14
  on goal setting, 78
  on listening, 34
Berlin, Irving, on success, 197
Berra, Yogi, 87
brainstorming, 153–154

Carlyle, Thomas, on seeing situation at hand, 160
Chandler, Walt
  on learning about company, 23
  on work performance, 182
chronological analysis, 154–155
coaching, 166
  development, 199
  performance, 182–185
coercive work environments, 68
communication, 2, 3, 18, 93–108
  barriers to effective, 93–94
  case studies involving, 98–102
  and credibility of speaker, 97–98
  and goal setting, 75–76, 87–90

and problem solving, 159
responsibility for effective, 97
and teamwork, 102–106
varying approaches to, 97
worksheet on, 107–108
see also feedback; listening
competence, 31
compliments, 104–105
confidence, with customers, 31
consistency, 40
continuous improvement, 162–164, 199
correspondence, answering, 51
cost-benefit analysis, 136–137
costs, limiting, 39–40
courtesy, with customers, 31
credibility, 97–98, 238
customers, expectations of, 26–33
customer service, 30–33

decision making, 127–144
  analytical approach to, 127–128
  case studies involving, 130–134
  collaborative approach to, 129
  cost-benefit approach to, 136–137
  delegating approach to, 129
  directive approach to, 128
  effective, 128–130

decision making (*continued*)
  group, 141–142
  individual, 134–141
  participative approach to, 128
  steps for, 134–143
  worksheet for, 144
delegation, 109–126
  barriers to, 111–112, 124
  benefits of effective, 111–114
  case studies involving, 114–117
  of decision making, 129
  definition of, 109
  and identification of tasks, 118–121
  and management style, 124–125
  and meetings, 123
  and sharing power, 110–111
  worksheets for, 121–122, 126
de Mille, Agnes, on decision making, 127
dependability, 32
development review, 197–201
  case studies involving, 202–212
Drucker, Peter
  on managing employees, 57
  on objectives, 76

E-mail, responding to, 50
employees
  delegating to, *see* delegation
  empowering, 109
  expectations of, 33–37
  face-to-face meetings with, 67
  protecting, 40
  resolving difficulties with, 160–162
  see also coaching; feedback
empowerment, 109

Evered, James F., on delegation, 109
example, setting a good, 47–51
expectations, 22–38
  case study involving, 35–37
  of customers, 26–33
  of employees, 33–37
  learning about, 22–23
  of management, 24–26
  and motivation, 70
  worksheet on, 38
expenses, limiting, 39–40

fairness, ensuring, 40
Federico, Cynthia, on learning about company, 23
feedback, 96–97, 166–188
  action steps for, 171–173
  case studies involving, 175–180
  descriptiveness of, 174–175
  goals of, 174
  guidelines for giving, 167–169
  and listening, 169–171
  performance, 182–185
  and progress reviews, 173–174
  use of root-cause analysis in, 180–182
  worksheet on, 186–188
  see also performance appraisal
force-field analysis, 155–156
Ford, Henry, on getting ready, 22
Frankl, Victor, on life mission, 1
Frost, Robert, 223
funneling, 75

Gardner, John, on organizational blindness, 157

Glasow, Arnold H., on being prepared for change, 157
goals/objectives, 74–92
  achievable, 79
  and anticipation of problems, 84
  benefits of setting, 76, 77
  case study involving, 85–87
  and communication, 75–76, 87–90
  continuous process of creating, 77–78
  measurable, 78–79
  monitoring, 79–80
  and planning, 85
  prioritizing, 80–84
  relevance of, 79
  thought process behind setting, 75
  worksheet for setting, 91–92
  writing down, 76–77
Goethe, Johann, on putting thoughts into action, 140
grievances, 45
group decision making, 141–142

halo effect, 190
Hillary, Sir Edmund, 233
Holmes, Oliver Wendell, on moving ahead, 77
Horan, John
  on decision making, 127
  on effective supervising, 14
  on listening, 34
horned effect, 190

Iacocca, Lee
  on ideas, 93
  on management, 166
individual decision making, 134–141
information power, 11

Kettering, Charles, on getting ahead, 9

language, use of appropriate, 47–48
learning
  about expectations, 22–23
  about policies and procedures, 42–45
listening, 33–35, 94–95
  and feedback, 169–171
  and problem solving, 159
Luce, Henry R., on business, 151

management
  establishing good relationship with, 53–54
  expectations of, 24–26
McCarthy, Michael F.
  on face-to-face meetings with employees, 67
  on learning by supervisors, 28–29
  on listening, 33
  on transition to supervisor, 18
McGregor, Douglas, on manager types, 124–125
measures, goal, 78–79
meetings, 214–231
  achieving results with, 224
  arriving on time for, 51
  barriers to effective, 214–216
  conducting, 221–229
  and delegation, 123
  disruptive behavior at, 222, 226–229
  face-to-face, with employees, 67
  gaining commitment at, 223–224
  guidelines for effective, 225–229

meetings (*continued*)
  hidden concerns with,
    219–220
  preparing for, 216–218,
    220–221
  when to have, 218–219
  worksheet for, 230–231
motivation, 57–73, 167
  case studies involving, 60–66
  creating environment for,
    67–69
  and productivity, 69–72
  and supervision style, 57–60,
    66–67
  worksheet on, 73
Mulroney, John P., on first line
  supervisors, 12

objectives, *see* goals/objectives
organizational culture, 49
  and motivation, 67–69

Percy, Charles, 238
performance appraisal, 189–213
  case studies of, 191–196,
    202–212
  definition of, 189
  development review as com-
    ponent of, 197–201
  objectivity of, 190
  pitfalls of, 190–191
  specificity of, 190
  worksheet for, 213
  see also self-assessment
performance coaching, 182–185
personal ability, and motivation, 70–71
personal power, 11
phone calls, returning, 50
planning
  and goal setting, 85
  for meetings, 216–218,
    220–221

policies/procedures, 39–56
  becoming informed about,
    42–45
  case study involving, 40–
    41
  goals of, 39–40
  and professionalism, 51–54
  and setting a good example,
    47–51
  for training, 45–47
position power, 11
power, 10
  effective use of, 12–15
  sharing, 110–111
  types of, 10–12
prioritizing, of goals/objectives,
    80–84
problem avoidance, 145, 146
problem solving, 145–165
  and anticipation of problems,
    84
  approaches to, 145–146,
    151–152
  with behavior/performance,
    160–162
  and brainstorming, 153–154
  case studies involving,
    146–151
  and chronological analysis,
    154–155
  and continuous improve-
    ment, 162–164
  and force-field analysis,
    155–156
  proactive approach to, 145–
    146, 156–160
  steps for, 152–153
  use of repetitive why work-
    sheet in, 155
  worksheet for, 165
process measures, 78–79
productivity, and motivation,
    69–72

professionalism, 51–54
progress reviews, 173–174

relationship power, 12
repetitive why worksheet, 155
resource power, 11–12
respect, showing, 31–32, 48
responsibilities of supervisors,
    4–5, 9–10, 15–19
results measures, 78–79
rewards, and motivation, 71
Rickover, Hyman G., 225
root-cause analysis, 180–182
Ruskin, John, on happiness in
    work, 188

self-assessment, 232–242
    and credibility, 238–239
    tool for, 233–238
    worksheet for, 240–242
self-monitoring, of goals/objec-
    tives, 79–80
Serviolo, Larry, on communica-
    tion, 18, 34
skills, supervision, 1, 5–7
    self-assessment of, 20–21
SMART, 78, 79, 91, 239
style, supervision, 57–60
supportive work environments,
    68–69

teamwork, and communica-
    tion, 102–106
Theory X managers, 124
Theory Y managers, 125
Thoreau, Henry David
    on achieving success, 232
    on being busy, 74
Toto, Joseph, on gaining
    commitment from others,
    69
training, policies and proce-
    dures for, 45–47
Truman, Harry, on decision
    making, 127–128

union contracts, 44
unwritten rules, 49, 52

Ward, Sandra M., on transition
    to supervisor, 2
Watson, Thomas J., Jr., on
    success of organizations,
    39
"we/they" language, 3
work environment, and motiva-
    tion, 67–69, 71–72
written rules, 52

Zitto, Johanna, on transition to
    supervisor, 15